H.G. WELLS' ASTOUNDING ADVENTURE IN DYNAMATION!
FIRST MEN IN THE MOON

OUT OF THE AGE OF WONDERS
—one of the most wonderful motion pictures of our time!

THE 7th VOYAGE OF SINBAD

in DYNAMATION · TECHNICOLOR

KERWIN MATHEWS · KATHRYN GRANT
RICHARD EYER · TORIN THATCHER

GREATEST ODYSSEY OF THE AGES!

JASON AND THE ARGONAUTS

TODD ARMSTRONG · NANCY KOVACK · GARY RAYMOND · LAURENCE NAISMITH

FROM THE TOP OF THE SKY TO THE BOTTOM OF THE SEA

plunging into adventure
beyond imagination
...a world beyond belief!

mysterious island TECHNICOLOR

Columbia Pictures presents a Charles H. Schneer production in Superdynamation starring Michael Craig · Joan Greenwood · Michael Callan · Gary Merrill · Beth Rogan and Herbert Lom as Captain Nemo

"The Beast From 20,000 Fathoms"

Roaring into Theatres Coast to Coast SOON!

the 7th Voyage of Sinbad

NOTHING LESS THAN A MIRACLE IN MOTION PICTURES!

COLUMBIA PICTURES presents

THE 3 WORLDS OF GULLIVER

in SUPERDYNAMATION and Eastman COLOR

starring KERWIN MATHEWS

JO MORROW · JUNE THORBURN

THIS IS 'THE ANIMAL WORLD'

TECHNICOLOR

2 BILLION YEARS IN THE MAKING!

WARNER BROS. CAMPAIGN

OUT-OF-SPACE CREATURE INVADES THE EARTH!

20 MILLION MILES TO EARTH

WILLIAM HOPPER · JOAN TAYLOR

MIGHTY JOE YOUNG

TERRY MOORE · BEN JOHNSON

Ray Harryhausen's
Fantasy Scrapbook

Ray Harryhausen's

Fantasy Scrapbook

Models, Artwork and Memories from 65 Years of Filmmaking

Ray Harryhausen and Tony Dalton

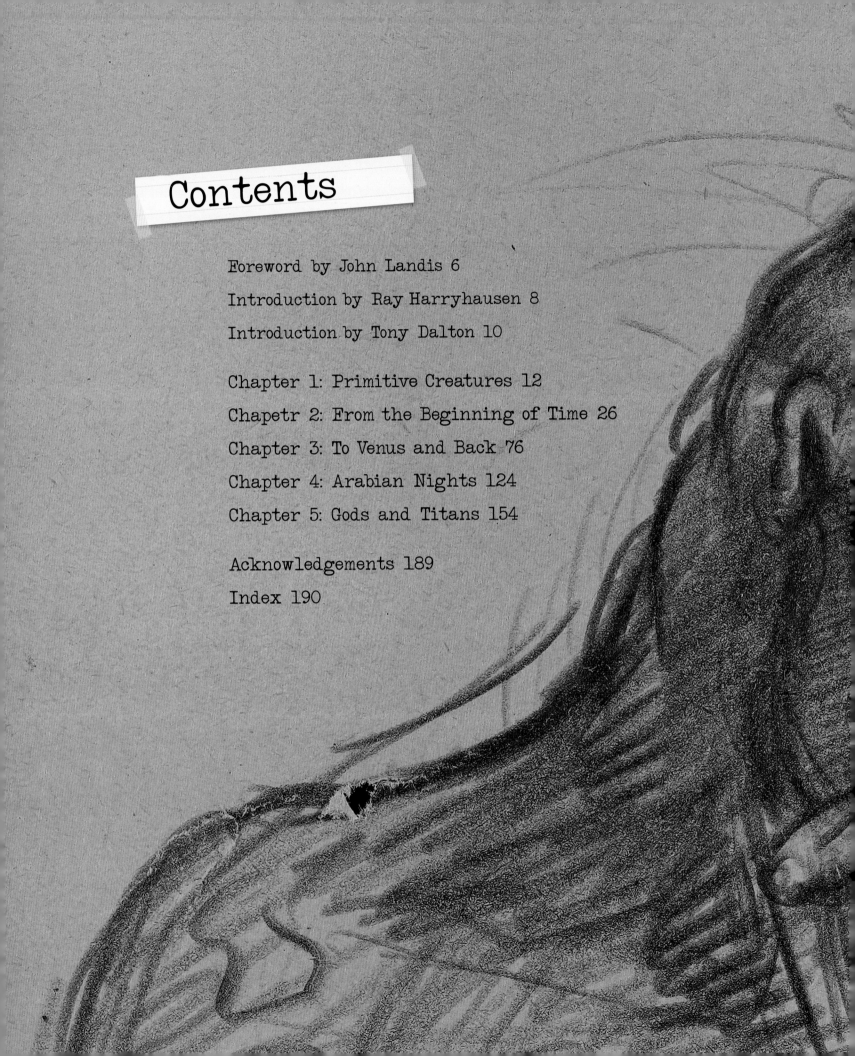

Contents

This book is dedicated to Ray
Harryhausen's parents, Fred and Martha,
who saw in their only child a rare
talent. Without them we wouldn't have
been privileged to witness so many
wonders. Also to Willis O'Brien and all
the technicians who work in many
small back rooms creating cinematic
life and wonderful entertainment.

Foreword by John Landis

Above: John Landis in the hands of the great master, ready for animation. Taken at The London Film Museum on 29 June 2010, Ray's 90th birthday and the opening of the London exhibition of his work.

It is my honor and privilege to be asked by Ray and Tony to write the Foreword to this wonderful book. A beautifully designed scrapbook of Ray's extraordinary and fantastic career, filled with unique treasures from his personal archives. Ray's beautiful daughter Vanessa and his good friends Jim Danforth and Randall Cook recently explored the long locked-up garage on Ray's California property in the Pacific Palisades. They uncovered even more of Ray's drawings, puppets, props, plans and correspondence, some of which had been in their cardboard boxes for over 50 years! This volume includes much of this newly discovered material, published for the very first time.

For Ray's 90th birthday celebrations in June 2010, I hosted a surprise tribute at the British Film Institute's Southbank Theater in London. Among those who shot special video greetings to project that night were George Lucas, Steven Spielberg, James Cameron, Guillermo Del Toro, Frank Darabont, Terry Gilliam, Tim Burton and Ray's lifelong friend, Ray Bradbury. Brilliant FX men Dennis Muren, Phil Tippett, Ken Ralston, Randall Cook and gifted makeup artist Rick Baker made the trip from California to pay homage to the Master in person. Actors, co-workers and many of Ray's countless admirers came from all over the world. Peter Jackson flew from New Zealand to present Ray with the Lifetime Achievement BAFTA Award.

That night Peter screened footage from the charming stop-motion films he made as a 14 year old, under the spell of the Harryhausen movies he adored. Peter's early efforts, and later great success, perfectly represent the profound influence Ray and his stop-motion creations have had on generations of filmmakers.

That night the audience sat enthralled as scenes from Ray's exceptional body of work were projected. Once more the Harryhausen creatures of fantasy appeared with that special spark of life and personality Ray gives to all of his characters.

This marvelous book provides a rare insight into the incredible amount of hard work that Ray invested in his films. It is indicative of Ray's artistry that it all plays so elegantly and effortlessly onscreen.

John Landis
Los Angeles, July 2011

Above: Detail from a first-generation image from *Jason and the Argonauts*, showing Jason and his warriors fighting five of the seven skeletons.

Introduction by Ray Harryhausen

Above: Ray standing in front of the 8-foot statue of Medusa at The London Film Museum.

Right: One of the earliest images of Ray as a baby, being lovingly held by his mother, Martha. The picture was taken by Ray's father, Fred.

This then is the final book, a scrapbook containing a selection of memories that relate to each of the films I have worked on over the years since I first saw that epiphany film *King Kong* in 1933, as a 13-year-old. That was almost 80 years ago!

Most of the items contained in this book will be new to fans. A few have been seen before but are now enhanced, so enabling us to tell the story and show the development of each project. There are some items I don't remember keeping and most of these were found in my LA garage several years ago. Who would have thought that the armatures for my brontosaurus and tyrannosaurus rex would still exist, and all those marionettes, my first attempts to make inanimate objects move. The latter are crude but then when we begin our experiments, crudity is part of the process of learning.

I receive many letters asking for advice on how to get into the field of special effects. Times have changed so rapidly and radically since my day, which it has to be remembered, was way before the advent of computers or CGI, that it is impossible for me to answer or help in any constructive manner. Today's young people must find their own way of creating their dreams, and I am sure it will not be an easy adventure for them. Tenacity and patience are the key words in any effort, both of which certainly applied to the seeking and finding of my own path in the filmmaking world of the 1930s – and beyond.

I hope that this volume will be seen to once again complement our other books but at the same time, stand up on its own.

I am proud that this book has been published, as I am with the preceding volumes and hope that the fans and those interested in good fantasy will enjoy it for the eclectic balance of artifacts, images and paperwork.

Ray Harryhausen,
London, July 2011

Above: An oil painting by Willis O'Brien and Byron Crabbe for *King Kong*. This was the earliest impression of Kong, shown as a slavering gigantic ape but with human features.

Introduction by Tony Dalton

Above: Tony setting up a copy of the Medusa at The London Film Museum in 2010.

Although Ray made a total of 16 features, every one of them, perhaps with the exception of *The Animal World*, is considered to be a classic, not only of the fantasy genre but in general cinematic terms. Ray's body of work is its own genre – a Harryhausen film – because there are no other films like them nor anyone quite like Ray. The design of the creatures and sets and the style of animation remain unique to Ray. Although most were made in the 1950s, 60s and 70s they remain as popular as ever – adventures in fantasy created when such tales were so much more straightforward and so much more exciting.

This book has been designed to chronicle Ray's experiments and each of his classic titles, and hopefully to supply new insights into how this exceptional man worked.

Ray has never thrown *anything* away. Whilst clearing out his LA garage in 2008, we found still more wonderful materials, ranging from artwork to armature drawings, from marionettes to armatured models and from armatures to miniature props. It was a goldmine of Harryhausen memorabilia that allows us to fill some (sadly not all) of the gaps in his career. In addition we also located much 35mm and 16mm footage that has never been seen before, including tests from his Fairy Tales, *The Beast From 20,000 Fathoms*, *20, Million Miles to Earth* and *The 7th Voyage of Sinbad*. And we didn't have to go all the way to LA to find artifacts: I am constantly discovering treasures in London, tucked away in the strangest places. Ray never did like filing.

In 1972 Ray compiled a book entitled *The Film Fantasy Scrapbook*. This new volume is not a copy of that in any way, but a compilation of images and documents that add immeasurably to the Ray Harryhausen story. And whereas the first book was laid out in chronological order, this new volume is organized thematically, covering first Ray's earliest experiments and animation, then looking at his work in the genres of prehistory, science fiction, legend and mythology.

The items you see in this book, along with everything else Ray has in storage, have now been secured for the future. The Ray and Diana Harryhausen Foundation, a charitable trust, now looks after the collection and Ray's enduring reputation, and will control the archive into the foreseeable future. Helping us in that mammoth task is the National Media Museum in Bradford, England, which is storing the collection for the Foundation. This will allow us to make artifacts available for exhibitions around the world and eventually enable students of Ray's work and cinema history to study many items at close quarters. It has been both Ray's and my great ambition to protect the collection for the future, as it is an almost complete résumé of the art of stop-motion model animation, as well as a unique window into Ray's life and career.

When Ray and I began our first book together twenty years ago we never dreamed that we would one day be working on a fifth. Perhaps this volume does now complete the story, but then again, depending on what we find in more undiscovered boxes, maybe not?

Tony Dalton
Isle of Wight, England, July 2011
www.rayharryhausen.com

Above: Ray's daughter, Vanessa Harryhausen, standing outside his LA garage. The clearance of this entire space was completed in only 5 days.

Below: Jim and Randy looking at reels of 35mm tests, dailies and outtakes, all of which have now been restored by Peter Jackson.

Above: Legendary animator and artist Jim Danforth and visual effects artist and technician Randy Cook go through some of the many boxes (in this case armatures).

Chapter 1

Primitive Creatures

Whenever Ray talks about his marionettes, early experiments and tests, aside from the Fairy Tales, he usually refers to most of them as being very crude. The reason for this is that he is a perfectionist. However, what now seems crude by Ray's standards is undoubtedly magic to the rest of us. Those early attempts at puppet making are a way of understanding how his young and imaginative mind was working as he attempted to bring inanimate objects to life.

He began with marionettes but soon realized that this form of movement was not realistic enough. The movements would never achieve what he had seen in *King Kong* – and *Kong* was the objective. With some effort he did discover how *Kong* had been made, by a technique known as stop-motion model animation. The creatures were models with complex skeletons, or metal armatures, inside latex-covered bodies. These models could be moved a fraction of an inch and, stepping back, the animator could expose one frame of film at a time in order to capture that minuscule movement. If the animator was good, and Ray was very good, then a smooth movement was achieved as each frame was shot, and when projected at normal speed it would appear to give 'life' to the model.

Young Ray had discovered his true vocation.

Throughout the mid to late 1930s and early 1940s Ray spent his time perfecting his art and at the same time searching for fantastic tales that he could visualize by means of stop-motion.

Marionettes

The period in which the teenage Ray experimented with marionettes, or string puppets, was to be of great benefit in helping him to understand model construction, costumes, miniature sets, and movement. Helped by his mother, Martha, and his father, Fred, amongst the marionette plays he created was his version of *King Kong*, which featured some of the creatures that existed on Skull Island alongside *Kong* – the tyrannosaurus rex, the brontosaurus and the pterodactyl. Other characters included a nightclub singer, a pair of Apache dancers, a robot and a Santa Claus. But by far the most significant to us today are the three marionette skeletons, of which only one now exists.

1 Ray's first attempt at reproducing King Kong. Although he had begun using marionettes before seeing the film in 1933, this would be the first time he had tried to emulate characters from a movie. This marionette is made of padded imitation fur with a papier-mâché face and feet.

2 The first of what would turn out to be a long line of brontosaurus, also inspired by the film *King Kong*. Assisted by his mother, Ray made this from a brown cloth padded with old rags and cotton.

3 Ray's wonderfully imaginative version of a tyrannosaurus rex, again influenced by *King Kong*.

4 Ray's version of the pterodactyl or pteranodon that terrorises Fay Wray in *King Kong*. The face and beak are made of wood and papier-mâché, whilst the talons are bits of wire.

5 Although not featured in *King Kong*, the triceratops was known to Ray through the paintings by the artist Charles R. Knight. Ray's version of the creature is made of papier-mâché and padded cloth.

6 One of the first creatures Ray created when he began working with marionettes. His junior high school English teacher encouraged his interest in string puppets and asked him to stage a short marionette play about 'Good English, Bad English'. Although we had thought there were only two characters, when this dragon was found in Ray's LA garage, Ray identified it as one of the devil's (Bad) helpers. This winged creature was cleverly articulated in wooden sections to create a snake-like movement.

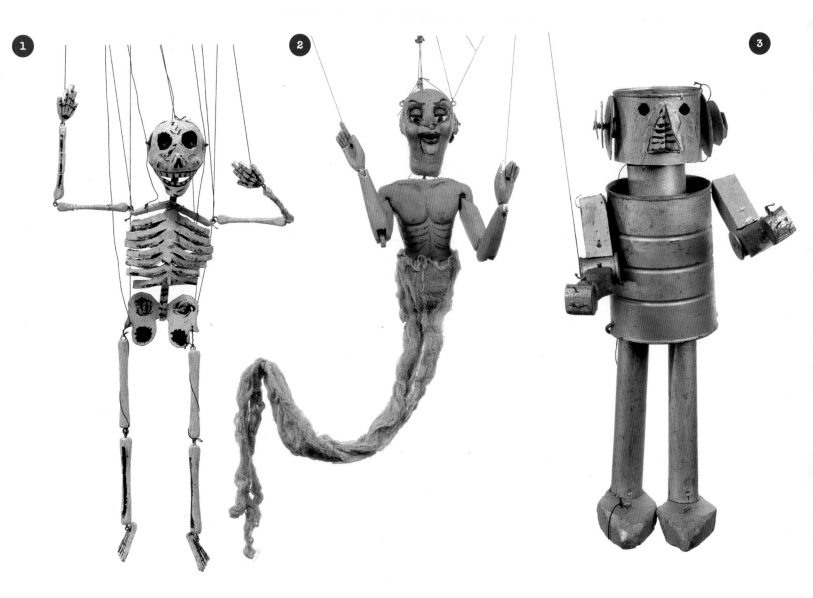

1 Ray's first 'living' skeleton. Again made of papier-mâché, the entire marionette comes apart like the dancing skeletons seen in Walt Disney's Silly Symphonies short *Skeleton Dance* (1928–29). Ray had been rather taken by the skeletons seen in the film, especially the sequence in which all their appendages flew apart.

2 A genie that would have appeared out of a bottle for an Arabian Nights story that Ray wrote for his marionette shows.

3 Always inspired by movies, this is Ray's version of a robot. Made out of tin cans, it evokes the era of the serials, for example *Flash Gordon* (1936) and *Buck Rogers* (1939).

4 Ray's marionettes became gradually more sophisticated, even though his passion for them had perhaps by now been replaced by armatured models and stop-motion. This beautifully made puppet represents the movie star Robert Taylor. The clothes were made by Ray's mother whilst the remainder of the puppet was made by Ray out of wood and resin.

5 A little earlier than the Taylor puppet, this Santa Claus was made for a Christmas play. Whilst the clothes were again made by his mother, the face and hands were made of papier-mâché by Ray.

6 One half of a pair of Apache dancers. Apache is a highly dramatic dance associated with Parisian street culture at the beginning of the twentieth century. This male dancer sports a knitted sweater, cloth trousers and a cap.

7 This simple but charming creature was influenced by a Disney film about a musical grasshopper in a top hat who plays a violin. Made completely of wood and carved by Ray, the violin and hat have since disappeared, as has the creature's right leg.

Fairy Tales

Prehistoric creatures would always be the main protagonists of Ray's early films but it was the series of colour Fairy Tales, which he began in 1945 and which he now calls his 'teething rings', that provided him with the opportunity to learn more about film-making. The first was a compilation of nursery rhymes under the banner *The Mother Goose Stories* (1946), followed by *The Story of Little Red Riding Hood* (1950), *The Story of Hansel and Gretel* (1951), *The Story of Rapunzel* (1952), *The Story of King Midas* (1953) and finally *The Story of the Tortoise and the Hare*, which he began in 1952 and completed 50 years later in 2002.

The Mother Goose Stories (1946)

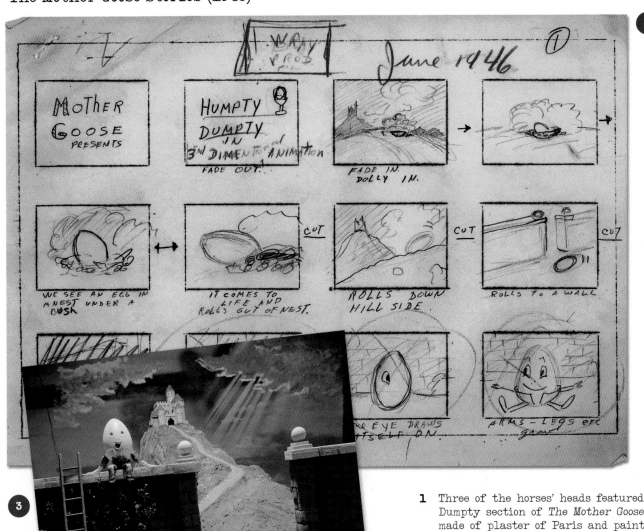

1 Three of the horses' heads featured in the Humpty Dumpty section of *The Mother Goose Stories* (1946), made of plaster of Paris and painted by Ray. He didn't have to make the horses' bodies as only the heads were seen in the film.

2 The rough storyboard, dated June 1946, for the Humpty Dumpty sequence. At the top of the page Ray has written 'Wray Prod', which became the production credit and would be used on the subsequent Fairy Tales.

3 A black and white shot of the final set and model used for the Humpty Dumpty sequence.

June 1946

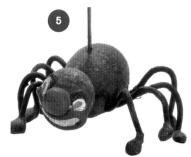

4 The first rough watercolour of the set for 'Little Miss Muffet' for *The Mother Goose Stories* (1946).

5 Recently uncovered in Ray's LA garage, this is the original spider model that scares Little Miss Muffet. Made of wood and suspended on a wire, which is still attached, this is one of Ray's most charming models.

6 The original model of Little Miss Muffet, again recently recovered from Ray's LA garage. Sadly she is not in the best condition, having been squashed in the bottom of a box.

7 Another of Ray's charming models made for *The Mother Goose Stories*. The Queen of Hearts was modelled after the film actress Marie Wilson, known as the 'dumb blonde'. Some of the Queen's movement was based on Bette Davis' very distinctive walk.

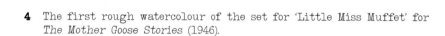

Queen of Hearts

1

2

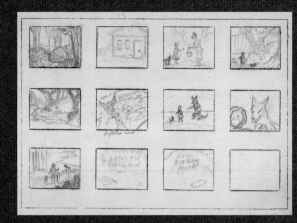

3

4

5

6

7

1 Ray's first design for Little Red Riding Hood, the Wolf and Riding Hood's little dog, which Ray dropped before beginning animation.

2 A page of a very rough storyboard for the film.

3-5 Three pencil sketches drawn on the back of photographic paper depicting key scenes and miniatures that would be seen in the final film. Again Red Riding Hood's dog is featured but because Ray would have had to create another animated model, which would have meant time and money, he left it out at an early planning stage.

6 Ray's original watercolour sketch of Little Red Riding Hood.

7 Perhaps the most complicated item in a stop-motion model is the metal armature. After Ray had designed the character he would set about detailing the construction of the armature, which had to be flexible enough for him to animate the model in precisely the way the story dictated.

8 A pencil sketch of Little Red Riding Hood's grandma in bed, drawn on the back of photographic paper.

9 The miniature set for Little Red Riding Hood's mother's house. Not only can some of the lights be seen, as well as the edge of a picture behind (probably one of Ray's designs for the film), but the underside of the animation table is also visible.

10 The metal armature (minus the arms) and one of the replacement heads, which Ray made himself, for the Little Red Riding Hood character.

11 The wolf minus his fur posed on Ray's parents' garden wall. Ray always built accurately where possible and here the latex body displays the ribs, which, when covered with the rubberized fur, would no longer be visible.

12 Ten plaster replacement heads, posed on Ray's parents' garden wall, for the Little Red Riding Hood model.

1

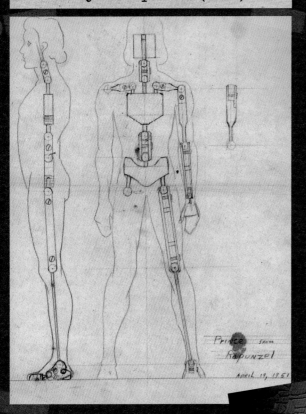

Prince FROM
Rapunzel

APRIL 19, 1951

2

3

4

5

1 The original armature drawing for the Prince featured in
   The Story of Rapunzel.

2 The original rough watercolour sketch for Rapunzel's tower
   and surrounding miniature set.

3 Rapunzel in her miniature tower, letting down her hair.

4 The miniature interior set of Rapunzel's tower room with
   the models of Rapunzel and the witch.

5 A rare image taken by Ray during the filming of the
   Rapunzel film, showing the miniature tower set and the
   edge of the background painting executed by Ray.

The Story of the Tortoise and the Hare (1952–2002)

6 A set of nine replacement plaster heads for the fox featured in *The Story of the Tortoise and the Hare*. The eye pupils (pieces of round blue paper from a hole punch) were added before animation. They were stuck to the eyes with wax and moved around with the eraser end of a pencil.

7 The complete model of the fox in his original costume made by Ray's mother. This was used in both the original footage shot in 1952 and again in the final shoot in 2002.

8 The original tortoise featured in the 1952 footage. Thought lost, it was remade for the 2002 photography, but this original was rediscovered in the LA garage.

9 The boys at work on the 2002 shoot. Ray (seated) with animator Mark Caballero standing behind watch fellow animator Seamus Walsh act out the hare's walk for the character's action.

The Adventures of Baron Munchausen (1950)

Inspired by Gustave's Doré's beautiful illustrations for *The Adventures of Baron Munchausen*, a book of fantastic tales, Ray began to design sequences for a film version in the late 1930s. In 1950 he shot some 16mm colour footage of the Baron talking to the Man in the Moon, for which he constructed a complex model. Sadly the project was unrealized.

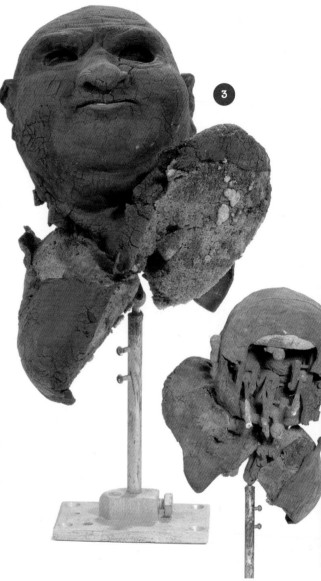

1-2 Eight separate storyboard drawings for *The Adventures of Baron Munchausen*. They relate to the Baron's encounter with the Man in the Moon.

3 Long thought lost, this is the model head and shoulders for the Man in the Moon, found in the LA garage. Now in poor condition, it was made of latex covering a system of levers designed to allow the model to talk. Ray had planned for the model to be synched with a recorded voice. However, after filming some test footage he discovered that this idea would take too long to realize.

Cave Bear (1935/36)

Ray's first 16mm filmed experiment using stop-motion was *Cave Bear*, which showed his model bear appearing from a cave and attacking humans. The model was constructed on a wooden frame, with the joints made of beads, and covered with his mother's fur coat. To the eager teenager it was a success and paved the way for more ambitious experiments.

1-2 The original Cave Bear model on a miniature set with a very basic articulated human model. The bear model was constructed of a wooden frame with the ball and socket armature made out of beads. It featured a moving tongue, claws and glass eyes.

3 A sketch in charcoal for a cave bear that would be featured in Ray's planned project *Evolution of the World* (see page 30), in which the huge creature would attack a tribe of animated cavemen.

4 Another charcoal and pencil sketch, of a caveman outside the Cave Bear's lair.

From the Beginning of Time

Like the great stop-motion pioneer Willis O'Brien (the creator of *King Kong*) before him, Ray discovered very early on that one of the best subjects for model stop-motion was prehistoric creatures. O'Brien had used them as central characters in his early comedy shorts and then brought them to life again in a more realistic manner for the 1925 film *The Lost World*. From there it was a short step to creating creatures such as Kong and the prehistoric inhabitants of Skull Island.

Like many youngsters, before and since, Ray was fascinated by dinosaurs. As a teenager he often visited the Los Angeles County Museum where various fossils were displayed and it was there that he also discovered paintings of dinosaurs by Charles R. Knight, who was to be an inspiration to Ray as he had been to O'Brien.

After the *Cave Bear* experiment Ray turned to more dramatic creatures such as an eyriops (his first model dinosaur), a stegosaurus (for which he won first prize at a competition held at the Los Angeles County Museum), a sloth, a pterodactyl, a brontosaurus, and a woolly mammoth. These, along with others, he placed in miniature dioramas in his parents' garden, and with a borrowed 16mm camera began the painstaking job of animating them walking across the screen and terrorising each other, as well as any humans that accidentally got in the way. By trial and error his animation skills developed and he slowly learned how best to build his models and how animals moved — even if they had been dead for 65 million years.

Early Dinosaur Experiments

Studying the fossilized bones and Charles R. Knight's paintings in his local museum, Ray set about creating a menagerie of prehistoric creatures. To begin with he built the models in his bedroom and animated them in miniature dioramas in his parents' garden, with little or no planning of the sequences he filmed. He also found that the sun moved as he meticulously animated his models in the garden. The result was that when the footage came back from the laboratory, the shadows also moved. As excited as he was at seeing his models 'move', the shadows destroyed the reality he was trying to create, so he moved into his father's garage. Now with his own studio, Ray soon discovered that an animator has to meticulously plan a scene and the action, so he began to make sketches and drawings of what he wanted his models to do on the screen.

1 A sketch, probably for an *Atlantis* storyline, showing a brontosaurus swimming towards an ancient city. Wherever he could, Ray would try to mix dinosaurs with legend.

2 Ray's second brontosaurus after his marionette version. The body was made of papier-mâché covered with a silk stocking. The neck armature was made of an articulated metal angle lamp.

3 The earliest image of the woolly mammoth (probably circa 1935), which Ray still has in his collection.

4 The stegosaurus that won first prize (Ray originally thought it had won second prize) in a competition at the LA County Museum. When Willis O'Brien saw the model he commented that the legs looked like sausages. Ray took his advice and went to anatomy classes.

5 One of Ray's earliest dinosaur models, the short-frilled and horned monoclonius (now known as the centrosaurus). It stands in a miniature set and was probably shot in Ray's parents' garden.

6 Ray's model dimetrodon with its 'sail' spine, again in a miniature set in the garden.

7 The monoclonius attacking a model human in the foreground.

8 A clipping from *Yank, The Army Weekly* magazine (circa 1940) about Ray's past experience, comparing his dinosaurs with the Nazi dinosaurs. Ray was not a private as indicated but a Sergeant 3rd Grade.

Schickelgruber's Noggin N.G.

Quick, now, what's the difference between a brontosaurus and a pterodactyl? Or are you a follower of the "Alley Oop" comic strip, too? No, we aren't going to report his creator has been drafted; but a boy who knows as much about prehistoric monsters as anyone—Pvt. R a y Harryhausen—is in the army to learn about modern monsters, of the flesh-and-blood as well as the purely mechanical type.

Pvt. Harryhausen, w h o s e hobby of modeling and photographing dinosaurs was featured in a recent issue of Popular M e c h a n i c, is forsaking the world of 1,000,000 B. C. to do his part toward eliminating some of the horrible hangovers from the caveman age, the new barbarians styling themselves "the Super Race."

Tyrannosaurus Rex was the terror of the world in his time," said Harryhausen, "but he had a large head with a small brain, and likewise his modern counterpart, "Tyranaseous" Schicklegruber, will die off."

Like the Dodo bird he will be come exstinked. Amen!

Evolution of the World (1938–40)

Ray began his first large-scale project in 1938, when he was seventeen. It was the very ambitious *Evolution of the World* that was intended to focus on the age of the dinosaurs until their demise 65 million years ago, resulting in the advent of mammals. Shooting on 16mm colour stock, Ray filmed sequences that included a fight between a tyrannosaurus rex and a triceratops as well as a brontosaurus swimming and then stepping onto land, which involved creating a matte of the water.

With this project he was learning the process of animation film-making. He carefully executed designs and drawings for the models and sets, and where possible followed a rough storyboard for what he hoped would work for the screen. His designs for the complex metal armatures were sketched well in advance, which enabled him to ensure the proper movement in the models that would be required for the sequence. He even began to make large key drawings of creatures to help him visualize the end results.

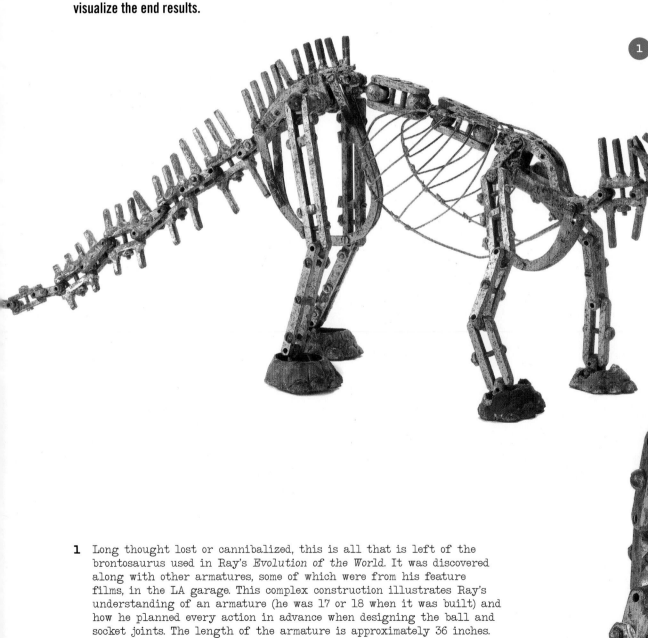

1 Long thought lost or cannibalized, this is all that is left of the brontosaurus used in Ray's *Evolution of the World*. It was discovered along with other armatures, some of which were from his feature films, in the LA garage. This complex construction illustrates Ray's understanding of an armature (he was 17 or 18 when it was built) and how he planned every action in advance when designing the ball and socket joints. The length of the armature is approximately 36 inches.

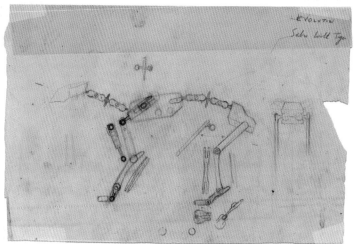

2 A copy of an original drawing of a carnivorous dinosaur. Probably a combination of a tyrannosaurus rex and an allosaurus, it was based on Charles R. Knight's drawings and paintings.

3 The armature design for a sabre-toothed tiger that would have featured in the project. As far as we know this was never built.

4 The armature design for a prehistoric ground sloth. Again this was never constructed for the project.

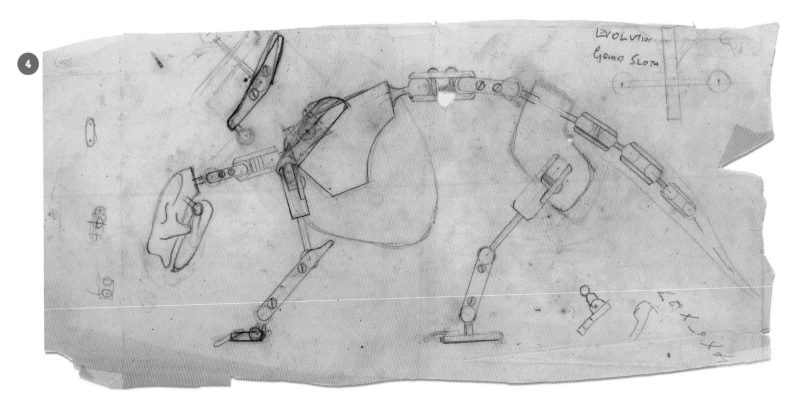

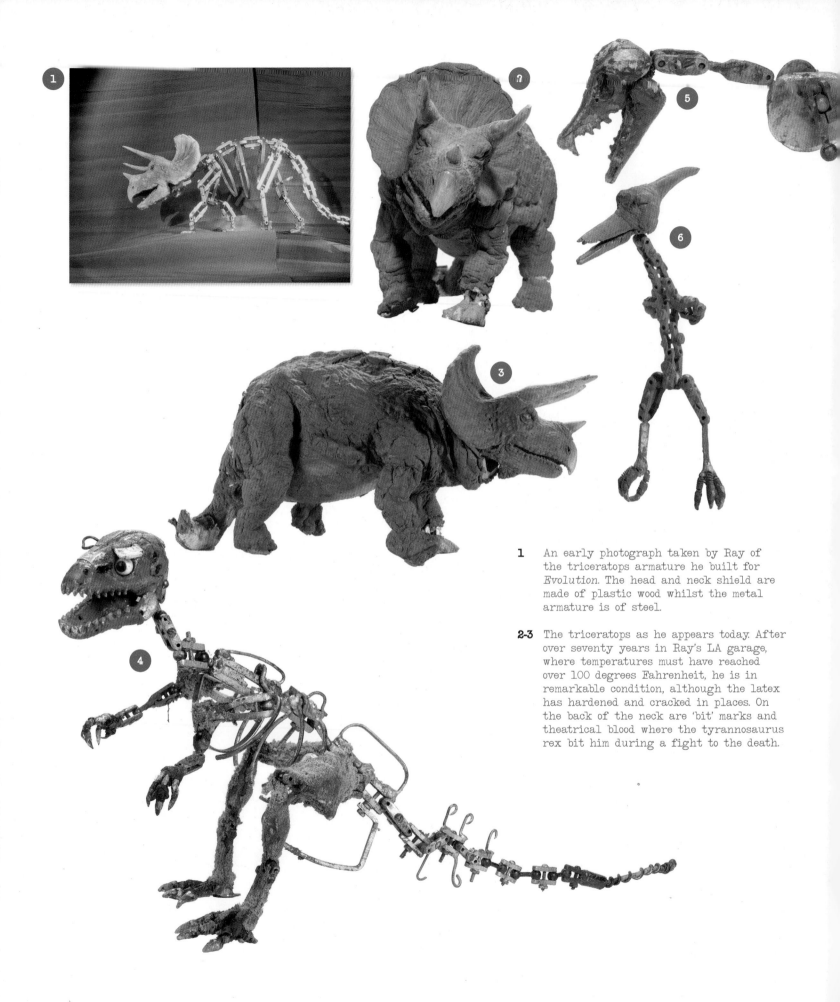

1   An early photograph taken by Ray of
    the triceratops armature he built for
    Evolution. The head and neck shield are
    made of plastic wood whilst the metal
    armature is of steel.

2-3 The triceratops as he appears today. After
    over seventy years in Ray's LA garage,
    where temperatures must have reached
    over 100 degrees Fahrenheit, he is in
    remarkable condition, although the latex
    has hardened and cracked in places. On
    the back of the neck are 'bit' marks and
    theatrical blood where the tyrannosaurus
    rex bit him during a fight to the death.

4 The armature for the tyrannosaurus rex which was built for the project (see image 7). Some sections of latex remain and the plastic wood head is still in good condition. This again demonstrates that Ray spent a great deal of time designing his complex armatures.

5 The armature head and neck for a camel, which Ray planned to feature in the project.

6 A partial armature for a pteranodon, distinguished by its head crest.

7 The tyrannosaurus rex stalks the brontosaurus within a miniature set built in Ray's hobby house studio, into which he moved after vacating his father's garage.

8 A wider view of one of Ray's miniature sets for *Evolution* in which he is animating his model monoclonius. He took great care to build his miniature vegetation, using bits of old wood and metal (often copper) for leaves.

9 The triceratops in its prehistoric set. Note the wooden aerial brace unit above the set. This was used to support the tyrannosaurus rex when it jumped on to the back of the triceratops.

10 The 18-year-old Ray carefully animating the triceratops.

Mighty Joe Young (1949)

Although it is not strictly a film about dinosaurs, *Mighty Joe Young* is a fitting addition to this chapter. After all it could perhaps be seen as Ray's *King Kong*.

In the 1940s Ray had worked with George Pal on his *Puppetoon* series, but his career as an animator was interrupted by the Second World War. After the war Willis O'Brien asked Ray if he would like to work on his new picture – *Mr Joseph Young of Africa*. He had no hesitation in saying yes.

What would become known as *Mighty Joe Young* was Ray's first experience in feature films. Working alongside his mentor O'Brien and other key figures on the *King Kong* production team it was a dream come true, and he carried out over ninety per cent of the animation.

Most of the artwork and test images in this chapter are from Ray's personal album, which he put together after the completion of the film.

1 A pre-production drawing by Willis O'Brien showing Joe pulling a rider from his horse. Even though this is a sketch, the detail in O'Brien's artwork is remarkable considering it was probably executed in a matter of minutes.

2 A test still from the film showing Joe pulling a rider off his horse. The rider would have been yanked from his animal by a wire and then Joe animated to correspond with the live action.

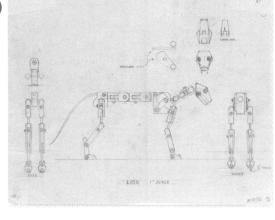

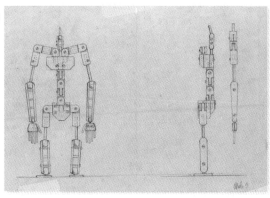

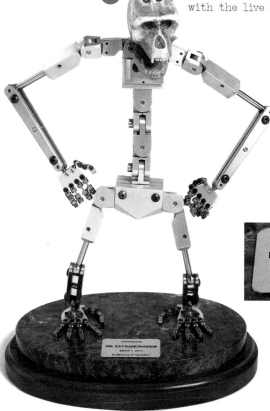

3 An original drawing by Ray for the lion armatures. O'Brien has written on the bottom right, 'make 3'.

4 Another original drawing by Ray, for the Joe armature. Although there were some changes this was the basic template for the final detailed armatures.

5 Ray always said that everyone had an armature of Joe but him. This is a new Joe armature built for Ray and based on one owned by friend and fantasy expert Bob Burns. It was commissioned by Jeff Taylor, who had four built. This is #1 and was presented to Ray in London on 1 March 2011 by Jeff. The plate says 'In Memory of "Jennifer"', the name by which Ray called his model of Joe.

1 Four watercolour pictures by Willis O'Brien for a sequence that was dropped from the final screenplay. This shows the main characters shipwrecked on an island on their way back from Africa. In it the lions attack the humans who are then saved by Joe.

2 Another dramatic black and white Willis O'Brien drawing of Joe fighting the lions on the island.

3 The cover of Ray's album commemorating the work on *Mighty Joe Young*. Drawn by production artist Mario Larrinaga, it shows the outside of the nightclub in which Joe will appear on stage.

4-6 Three wonderful watercolours by Willis O'Brien showing some of the planned scenes for the film. The only one that doesn't appear in the film is Joe pulling on the stage curtain (image 6).

MAX
O'HARA'S
GOLDEN SAFARI
STARRING
M? JOSEPH YOUNG
OF AFRICA

1   A drawing by Willis O'Brien for the lion cage sequence. This was to change from Joe holding the cage above his head to Joe pushing the cage over and the lion escaping.

2   A test to match the lion with the background glass painting. The underside of the animation table can just be seen.

3   Joe peering into the lion cage. Ray executed all of this sequence, which took him four days to complete. Afterwards one of the producers, no less a figure than director/producer John Ford, congratulated him on the effectiveness of the sequence.

4 Joe just about to have his fingers snapped at by the lion. Willis O'Brien photographed the lion at Thousand Oaks Lion Park and Ray animated Joe to correspond with the lion's actions.

5 A dramatic test shot of Joe during the roping sequence.

6-8 Three tests for the scene in which Joe looks at some caged chickens. The chickens were inserted in the same manner as the lion in the cage. Joe was first of all animated with a black card in the cage. The film was wound back and the black card was replaced with a white card and no lights. It was onto this card that the lion and the chickens were projected.

1 Another drawing by O'Brien, this time for the orphanage sequence. Here we see Joe clutching a number of children but in the final screenplay there is only one child to save.

2 The burning six-foot high miniature orphanage building.

3 A final cast and crew listing on which Merian C. Cooper has written 'God bless him!' next to Ray's name.

God bless him!

"MIGHTY JOE YOUNG"

EFFECTS PERSONNEL:

CHIEF TECHNICIAN: Willis H. O'Brien
FIRST TECHNICIAN: ✗Ray Harryhausen✗
SECOND TECHNICIAN: Pete Peterson
ASST. TECHNICIANS: E.B. Gibson
      Carl Gibson
CEL ANIMATION: Scott Whitaker

MINIATURES DRAFTSMAN: George C. Webb
ANIMAL CONSTRUCTION: Marcel Delgado
SPECIAL PROPERTIES: Victor Delgado
ANIMAL TAXIDERMIST: George Lofgren
ARMATURE CONSTRUCTION: Harry Cunningham
PAINTING TECHNICIAN: Peter Stich

CHIEF MATTE ARTIST: Fitch Fulton
ASST. MATTE ARTIST: Lou Lichtenfield
ASST. MATTE ARTIST: Vernon Taylor
ASST. MATTE ARTIST: Jack Shaw
SKETCH ARTIST: Widhoff

DIRECTOR OF PHOTOGRAPHY: Bert Willis
PROCESS CINEMATOGRAPHY: Harold Stine
ASST. EFFECTS CAMERAMEN: Monroe Askina
      Pinky Arnett
      Richard DeVol
      George Hollister
      Robert Touyarot
      Tex Wheaton
CHIEF ELECTRICIAN: Orville Beckett
CHIEF LAB TECHNICIAN: John Swain
OPTICAL EFFECTS: Linwood G. Dunn
      Cecil Love
OPTICAL CONSULTANTS: Consolidated Film Industries
MECHANICAL EFFECTS: Jack Lannon

*

PRODUCTION PERSONNEL:

PRODUCERS: John Ford
      Merian C. Cooper
DIRECTOR: Ernest B. Schoedsack
ORIGINAL STORY: Merian C. Cooper
SCREENPLAY: Ruth Rose Schoedsack
DIRECTOR OF
PHOTOGRAPHY: J. Roy Hunt
FILM EDITOR: Ted Cheesman
SOUND EDITOR: Walter G. Elliot
SOUND TECHNICIANS: John L. Cass
      Clem Portman
ART DIRECTOR: James Basevi
ASST. ART DIRECTOR: Howard Richmond
MUSICAL SCORE: Roy Webb
ORCHESTRATIONS: Constantin Bakaleinikoff

PARTICULARS:

RUNNING TIME: 96 MIN.
RELEASE DATE: July 30, 1949
FIRE SEQUENCE: Technicolor stock, tinted red & yellow
STUDIO: RKO-PATHE

A John Ford-Merian C. Cooper Presentation
An ARKO Production
An ARGOSY Picture

PREVIOUS TITLES:

MR. JOSEPH YOUNG
MR. JOSEPH YOUNG OF AFRICA
THE GREAT JOE YOUNG
THE MIGHTY JOE YOUNG

*

STUDIO MANAGER: Walter Daniels
UNIT PRODUCTION
MANAGER: Lloyd Richards
ASSISTANT DIRECTOR: Samuel Ruman
DIALOGUE COACH: Dixie McCoy
STUNT DIRECTORS: David Sharpe
      Cliff Lyons
DANCE DIRECTOR: Chas. O'Curran
SET DECORATOR: George Atwills
COSTUMES: Adele Balkan
MAKEUP: Mel Berns
TERRY MOORE'S MAKEUP: Harry Raye
HAIR STYLIST: Larry Germain
ASST. TO MR. COOPER: Zoe Porter
ANIMAL TRAINER: Mel Koontz

4

PRELIMINARY BUDGET DETAIL
LABOR AND MATERIAL

PICTURE NO. 2121
ACCT. NO. Animation

PICTURE TITLE MR. JOSEPH YOUNG

BUDGET REF. NO.	DESCRIPTION	DAYS, WEEKS OR QUANTITY	RATE	AMOUNT	SUB-TOTAL
	4 Projectors @ $4,000			16 000 00	
	4 Air condensers @ $75.00			300 00	
	4 Lenses @ $200.00			800 00	
	6 Stop-motion mach. $650.00			3 900 00	
	4 Tripods $200.00			800 00	
	Labor and Material for......				
	4 Gorillas 1 inch scale				
	4 Gorillas 1½ inch scale				
	2 Horses 1 inch scale				
	2 Men 1 inch scale				
	2 Men 1½ inch scale				
	2 Lions 1 inch scale				
	2 Lions 1½ inch scale				
	1 ea. plaster models of above......				
	1 Full size arm and hand of Gorilla.			4 000 00	
	20 Glasses (mounted)			1 500 00	
	31 Glass paintings @ $800.00 ea.			24 800 00	
	Material for Miniature sets			5 200 00	
	Proj. Screens			500 00	
	Paints & Brushes			500 00	
	Misc.			1 000 00	
	Dark room equipment			1 000 00	
	Roping mechanism			2 000 00	
					52 300 00

mounting $25.00 ea.

4 A Preliminary Budget sheet for production 2121, then called *Mr Joseph Young*. It shows the proposed budget for equipment, models and miniatures for the animation work.

5 'Young Harry', as O'Brien called Ray, with cameraman Bert Willis.

6 Willis O'Brien working on the miniature set for the roping sequence.

7 Left to right: the editor, Ted Cheesman, a worried Willis O'Brien and a very relaxed Merian C. Cooper, during live-action photography.

8 Willis O'Brien on set. O'Brien was one of the great pioneers of model stop-motion animation. Realizing this, Merian C. Cooper presented him with the Oscar that *Mighty Joe Young* won for Best Special Effects in 1950, in recognition of his work on the picture, and of course on *King Kong*, as the Academy had no category for effects when that film was released.

The Beast From 20,000 Fathoms (1952)

The Beast From 20,000 Fathoms was Ray's second movie and represented a major advance in his techniques. He was brought to the project when producers Jack Dietz and Hal Chester were trying to put it together as an independent production under their company Mutual Films. Ray persuaded Dietz that stop-motion would be a better way of bringing the creature to life than using a man in a rubber suit or live lizards with fins stuck to their backs, which is what had originally been proposed.

Whilst the screenplay was being fleshed out, Ray was faced with the task of putting the creature into the live action. For *Mighty Joe Young*, Willis O'Brien had sandwiched the model in miniature sets between glass paintings to create depth. This process would be far too expensive for the new project so Ray, using a split-screen technique he had long had in mind, made various tests to prove it would work. Ray's career had reached a crucial crossroad. Fortunately the technique worked and the split-screen process, later to become known as Dynamation, was born. The picture was a runaway success.

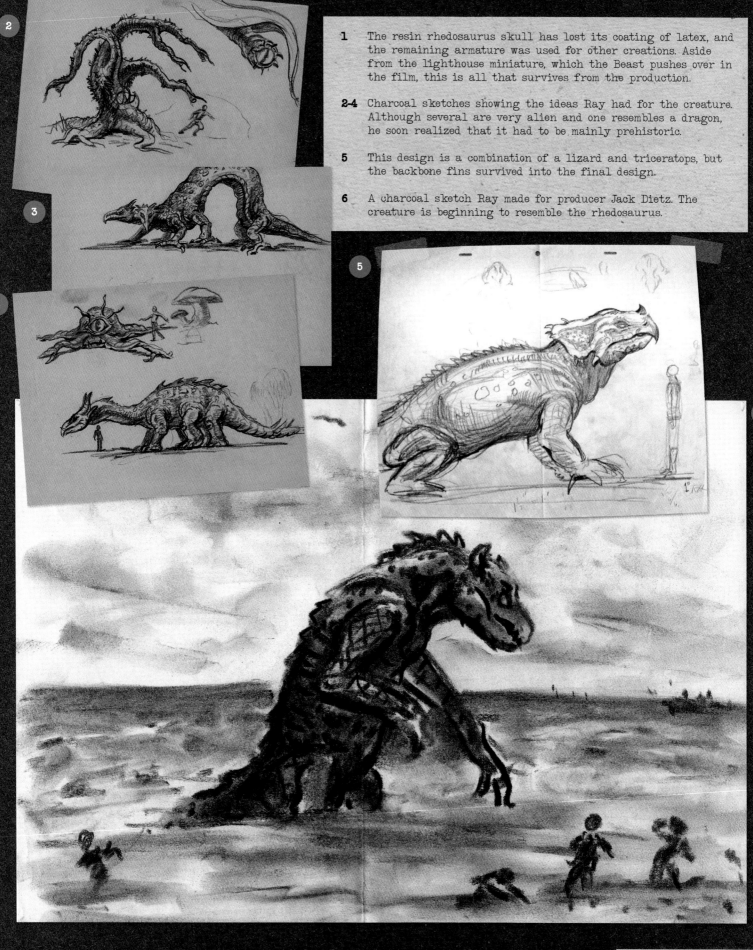

1 The resin rhedosaurus skull has lost its coating of latex, and the remaining armature was used for other creations. Aside from the lighthouse miniature, which the Beast pushes over in the film, this is all that survives from the production.

2-4 Charcoal sketches showing the ideas Ray had for the creature. Although several are very alien and one resembles a dragon, he soon realized that it had to be mainly prehistoric.

5 This design is a combination of a lizard and triceratops, but the backbone fins survived into the final design.

6 A charcoal sketch Ray made for producer Jack Dietz. The creature is beginning to resemble the rhedosaurus.

1

2

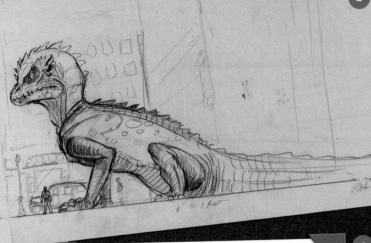

4

3

5

1 Aside from the ears, this design for the beast has a great many of the traits that the final creature would possess. The size too has increased.

2 The final drawing for the creature before Ray made his prototype model. Note that the head is still not quite what we now see as the rhedosaurus.

3 The first armature drawing.

4 A test with the first model of the beast within a photographic setup of the New York streets.

5 The model on the animation table. Ray decided that it didn't look viscious enough to destroy swathes of New York, so he set about fine-tuning the model, especially the head, which he made much more lizard-like.

Dynamation – The Split-Screen Process

Although simple in terms of film making, the split-screen process, which enables animated models to interact with live action, is difficult to relay in writing, so we have broken the technique down into basic stages. The name Dynamation was coined by Charles Schneer, who produced many of Ray's films.

1 To begin with the live action is planned by the animator so that when it is photographed the human actions will fit with the animation effects, which are done much later in the studio. The animator will have decided at this stage where he will optically spilt the screen.

2 The live-action, or rear-projection, plate is projected onto a rear-projection screen from behind. In front of this is placed an animation table on which the model(s) will be animated to interact with the live action on the plate.

3 In front of the animation table is placed a sheet of clear, clean glass in a wooden frame and again, in front of this is placed the stop-motion camera.

4 The animator looks through the camera viewfinder, and, in Ray's case, using a long stick with a china pencil taped to the end (a grease pencil used in editing), draws a line on the glass where he had planned to split the screen during the live-action shoot. Often this is along a convenient edge or around rocks or a hill. This in effect splits the screen in two.

5 The lower section of the glass (below the china pencil mark) is painted out with black matt paint.

6 The animator animates his model, or models, to correspond with the live-action plate one frame at a time.

7 Once this is complete, the film is run back in the camera. The glass is replaced by another piece of exactly the same size, on which the upper section is matted out with black paint. The rear projector is then run one frame at a time so that the camera has now recorded both sections of the live action.

The end result is that all three elements – the lower and top sections of the screen and the animated model or models – are seen as one, so giving the illusion of a huge beast being actually part of the live action.

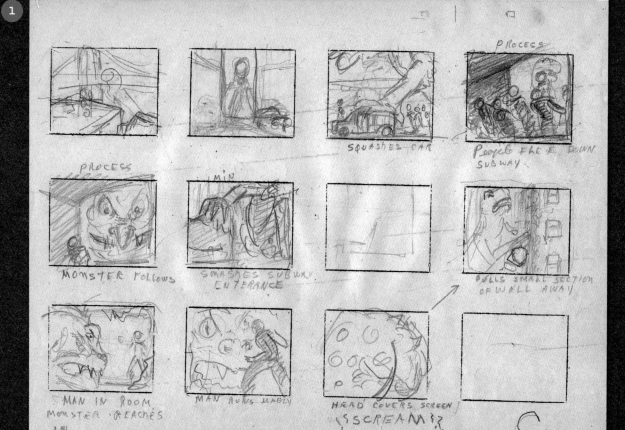

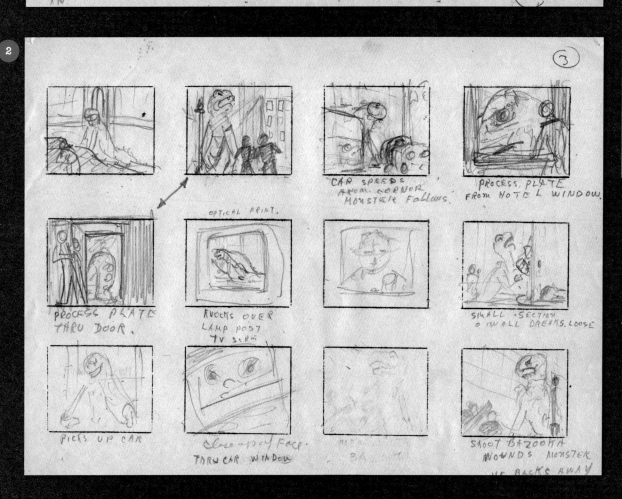

1-2 Two pages of a rough and incomplete storyboard that Ray executed for a section of the Beast's rampage through New York. These two pages were the only storyboards that he managed to compose.

3-10 A selection of test frames taken from the footage discovered in Ray's LA garage. They are therefore first-generation quality.

3 The rhedosaurus in the Arctic. The human in the fur coat in the foreground is one of the film's producers, Hal Chester, who was photographed against black then printed into the picture by means of an optical printer.

4 A close-up of the Beast showing its forked tongue.

5 The most famous scene in the film – the creature pushing over the lighthouse on the rock promontory.

6 A full-on shot of the Beast on the New York streets.

7 The rhedosaurus animated within the miniature of the roller coaster.

8 A high shot of what will be the rhedosaurus on the street. The area blacked out is the matte into which the creature will be animated and placed.

9 The composite shot of 8 showing the creature inserted.

10 A very rare shot; Ray doesn't remember filming this at all. Although the elements – the lighthouse and the headland – are as they are seen in the final film, the creature has emerged from the left of the lighthouse and not the right. In the test footage this scene only lasts for a matter of seconds so Ray must have quickly decided that it would work better from the right.

THE MONSTER FROM UNDER THE SEA

1. During the preparation for the explosion and the allied news coverage scenes, the many queries to scientists, etc., we meet our principals. BOBBY (ROBERTA GREENLY), JOHN HERALD and DR. LATHROP, stoic genius, supermind in the field of robots and differential analyzers (electronic brain). Lathrop predicts that the explosion will tear through the earth's core, out will reseal itself rapidly. In this SEQUENCE we plant the following. Bobby's familiarization with COSMIC AND CELESTIAL time charts. HERALD, admirer of LATHROP tries to emulate his unemotional philosophy. Also establish the things that a robot of the future can do.

2. THE EXPLOSION - Intercutting with STOCK STUFF of cascading oceans, etc., is our trio at the lab. Dr. Lathrop has mapped by radar the tear in the earth's surface, and before our eyes we see it reseal itself -- but during the resealing there is a terrific shudder, coming a full three hours after the explosion. Use same diving business - the heat, the ruined instruments.

3. SMALL FISHING BOAT SEQUENCE, in which the monster observes the Portugese fishermen. Fishermen sweat. They send out a call to whale boats about the big 'fin' they saw. MONSTER VANISHES -- appears in middle of whaling fleet. They try to harpoon it. The fleet is destroyed. Steam, clouds, rain, squall. Thermals. Actual change in climatic conditions for an area of two miles.

4. REACT ON - The small fishing boat arrives in port. The crew is amazed to learn of destroyed whale fleet. People generally accept it as a flash storm. First ring of doubt comes as the fishermen haul their fish aboard into market. Spoiled! Radioactive!

5. BOBBY-HERALD-RICH...get the facts. First [...] fleet disaster is that it was caused by [...] core material - highly radioactive. T[...] felt three hours following the initi[...] the piercing of the SONO-BAND made u[...] from miles of water above it, and th[...] force from the earth's core. This b[...] earth. Snapped at any point, its re[...] almost simultaneously all over the e[...] measured strength to break it. Appa[...] just that. Bobby and Herald disagre[...] in accord regarding an examination o[...] core, to ascertain the extent of the [...]

12.

124. They interview the soldier who fired the bazooka.

125. Newspaper headlines in French, German, Japanese, Russian, Arab, all say the same thing, "Monster dead."

126. A scientist announces a new theory of evolution based on the re-birth of the monster.

127. A line of men forms in front of a store counter eagerly buying hand-painted neckties, decorated with pictures of the monster.

128. A manufacturer turns out monster sweat shirts for little monsters.

129. Kids buy the new monster gun, modelled after the bazooka.

130. Tom and the meeting scientists say they'd be much happier if they could see the dead body. They have had to block off the section of New York where the monster bled. Hundreds of people who were there are running high fevers. A messenger rushes in. Tom is wanted right away.

131. The President is throwing out his new chief of staff, as Tom enters. What's wrong? The phone rings. Another report.

132. On the other end of the phone a reporter hangs up and runs.

133. The monster is coming up a country road. Dogs bark at him. Cats hunch their backs and snarl.

134. A farmer leaves his hay wagon and runs for his life.

135. Sheep turn and run away. Cows panic and trot off.

136. The monster tears down a chicken house. The hens run away in panic.

1-2 Two pages from the rough outline for the film, which was then called *The Monster From Under the Sea.*

3 A cartoon of Ray and his creature by producer Hal Chester.

Ray's initial scribbled notes on costs for equipment and miniatures.

5-6 When the film was sold to Warner Bros by Dietz and Chester, the new owners not only had a new score written but went to town with the publicity, making it one of the most successful films of 1952. These are two pages from the exhibitors' publicity campaign brochure.

NEWS FLASH

PREHISTORIC BEAST ATTACKS!

City Ripped by Raging Sea-Giant From Ages Past!

It's alive!

Science is ama...
They cou...
And...

WARNER BROS. ZEIGEN:

PAUL
**CHRISTIAN-
HUBSCHMID**

PAULA RAYMOND

CECIL KELLAWAY

KENNETH TOBEY

JACK PENNICK

in

Panik in New York

(THE BEAST FROM 20,000 FATHOMS)

STREET BALLYS!

24-SHEET TRUCK

The "beast" is 8-feet high on the 24-Sheet! Just right for an advance truck bally!

Footprints!....

1) For display out front. Have local plasterer model a full-scale clay mold of a large footprint — copy from ads. Mold is encased in a box with the dimensions of the print measuring 36 inches across circumference and 18 inches deep. Spray with gray paint to simulate clay and post sign which reads: "This FOOTPRINT was left by 'THE BEAST FROM 20,000 FATHOMS'!"

2) Cover the sidewalks of main streets with huge footprints of beast painted in a trail leading to your boxoffice. Footprints bear copy "Soon! 'The Beast From 20,000 Fathoms'."

SEND THE SPECIAL 10-FOOT DISPLAY AROUND TOWN!

The Special 10-Foot Animated Display can also be used to good effect away from your theatre. Prop it up on the back of a flat truck, banner the sides, and have it driven around town for several days before it goes back into your lobby.

Street Snipe

THE 'BEAST'
IS COMING!

USE YOUR FRONT!

For a flash front!—cut out and mount the beast from the 24-sheet. Set it up high on the marquee! Under the marquee use the fluorescent satin valances offered by the National Flag Co. Sketch also shows use of the 40 x 50 "See" display easily assembled by your artist.

Page Nineteen

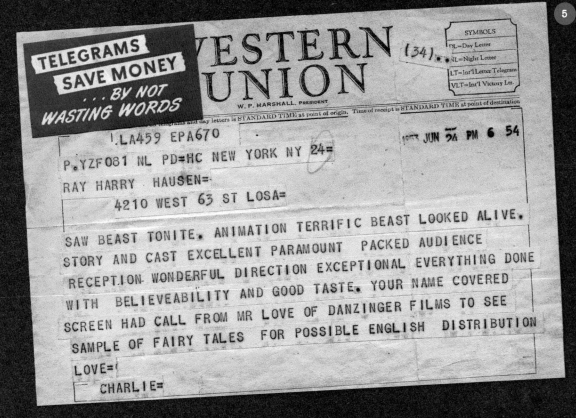

The Animal World (1956)

Ray's next prehistoric subject, an Irwin Allen production called *The Animal World*, is not one of his favourites. Apart from working again with his mentor Willis O'Brien, which was the main reason he chose to work on the project, he had little input into the design of the creatures or the action. Alongside O'Brien, who planned the setups, Ray carried out all the animation for the dinosaur section of the film, which recounted the age of the dinosaurs and their demise. It wasn't dissimilar to Ray's earlier idea for *Evolution of the World* and in fact Allen had Ray's 16mm footage for that project enlarged to 35mm for possible use. However, because Ray had shot that footage at 16 frames per second, the action was speeded up when projected on 35mm, so it was decided to start from scratch.

1 A publicity shot of Irwin Allen (centre) talking to a staff member from the Warner Bros miniature department about the armatures.

2 One of the pages from the US publicity brochure produced by Warner Bros (the cover and another page can be seen opposite). It features an item called 'Shooting The Animal World with Camera', which is full of inaccuracies, the most glaring being the claim that Navy jets were discovered in the sky whilst reviewing the footage of the dinosaur fight. In fact the backgound for the dinosaur animation was painted. Also the eggs for the baby brontosaurus scene were miniature plaster eggs and not real ones as suggested in the piece.

3 Three armatures for the film built by the Warner Bros miniature department. It is difficult to establish which creatures they turned into but the middle one is almost certainly the brontosaurus.

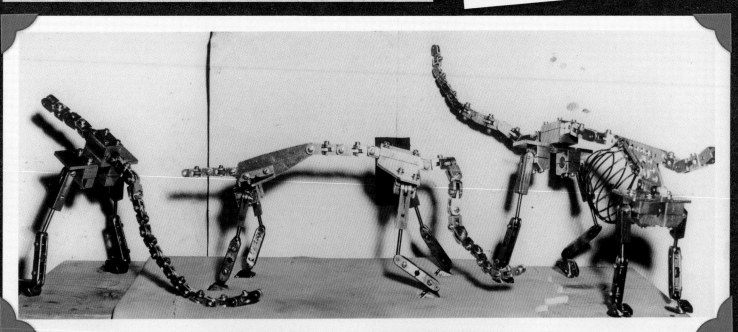

One Million Years B.C. (1966)

It would be 10 years before Ray was given the opportunity to work on another pure prehistoric film that featured dinosaurs. Loaned out to Hammer Films by Morningside Productions (producer Charles Schneer's production company), Ray designed the effects and dinosaurs for *One Million Years B.C.*, a loose remake of the 1940 movie *One Million B.C.* (aka *Man and His Mate*), which had used men in rubber suits and real lizards for the dinosaurs.

Ray thought the basic storyline of a caveman meeting a cavewoman was slight, but he knew he could improve on the effects and make them, aside from Raquel Welch and her fur-trimmed bikini, the stars of the film. It was a huge international success and continues to be one of Ray's most popular films.

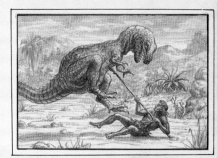

1 The original armatured model of the allosaurus.

2 A set of four pencil drawings by Ray for the allosaurus' attack on the shell people's camp. Although Ray executed a storyboard for most of the major animation scenes in his movies, he occasionally produced a small set of drawings as an initial aid for the screenwriters.

3 A rough pencil sketch of the death of the ceratosaurus.

4 One of the many key drawings Ray produced for *One Million Years B.C.* This shows the allosaurus attacking the camp.

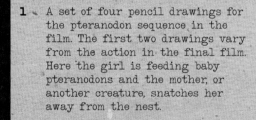

1 A set of four pencil drawings for
the pteranodon sequence in the
film. The first two drawings vary
from the action in the final film.
Here the girl is feeding baby
pteranodons and the mother, or
another creature, snatches her
away from the nest.

2 Rough pencil sketches by Ray
for the pteranodons, including a
delightful drawing of one of the
babies and its egg.

3 A test still from the aerial
fight between the pteranodon and
pterodactyl, during which the
former drops the small model of
Raquel Welch into the sea. Only
just visible above the left-hand
model are two wires supporting it.

4 Ray's key drawing of the
pteranodon snatching the girl.

5-11 Various location recce photographs taken by Ray in Lanzarote in the Canary Islands. Ray used these for planning his storyboards and working out the action that would appear in the Dynamation sequences.

5-6 These images show the film's director, Don Chaffey, on location. In image 6 Ray has sketched in steam above a possible volcano and what looks like shrubs or perhaps dinosaur tracks in the lower half of the picture.

7-11 Various other recce shots including three images on which Ray has sketched steaming volcanoes and pterodactyls to assist him in visualizing the scenes.

1 A set of eight pencil drawings of the proposed attack of a brontosaurus on the rock people. Sadly this sequence was dropped from the final screenplay and the brontosaurus appears in the film only briefly, in a wide shot walking left to right. The image of a gigantic head reaching into the safety of the cave was one that intrigued Ray as a dramatic cinematic experience.

2-5 Four more location recce shots, on two of which Ray has sketched in the proposed death of the brontosaurus as it sinks into a lava basin. Image 4 again features Don Chaffey, enacting a possible pose.

6 Ray's original and initial sketch for the giant archelon featured in the film.

ARCHELON

RH

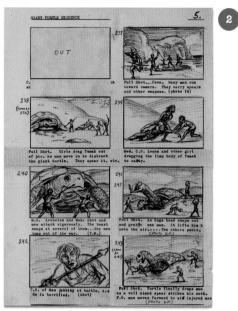

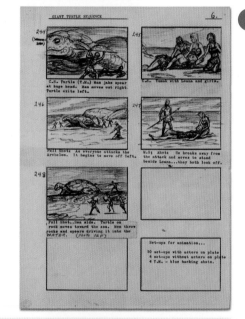

1-3 Three pages of the storyboard for the archelon sequence. This demonstrates, as do most of Ray's storyboards, just how much advanced planning went into his animation sequences and how little, if anything, was wasted.

4 Four pencil drawings showing Ray's initial ideas for the archelon sequence. In this version Tumak is drifting into the shore on some wood and is attacked by the archelon. In the final version Tumak collapses on the beach and is in the way of the advancing archelon.

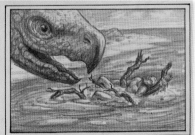

5-8 Four recce photographs of the Playa Blanca location, onto which Ray has drawn some of the archelon action.

PLAYA BLANCA

9 A rare set of four pencil drawings on yellow paper of the planned but unrealized sequence that would have preceded the attack of the allosaurus on the shell people camp. After *Mysterious Island* Ray had always wanted to animate another phororhacos (now usually called a phorusrhacos). These drawings show the poor creature being chased from the camp and attacked by the allosaurus. However, Ray never wasted a good idea. In *The Valley of Gwangi* the ornithiminus introduces Gwangi in exactly the same manner.

1.

REVISED OUTLINE

ONE MILLION B.C.

May 21, 1965

I. PROLOGUE
   A. Titles

II. PREHISTORIC INTRODUCTION SEQUENCE
   A. Fight with small animal.
      1. Eating scene
      2. Father drives son out of cave.
      3. Mammoth pursues Tumak to river and cliff.
      4. Tumaks fall into river.

III. TUMAKS RIVER JOURNEY
   A. Possibly go down some rapids.
   B. Floats through jungle with mild prehistoric animals in B.G.
      1. Floats to mouth of river and drifts into nearby lagoon

IV. INTRODUCTION OF LOANA
   A. Loana and girl friend spearing fish in other nearby Lagoon.
      1. Loana sees branch with man clinging to it bobbing near rocks. Moves closer.
      2. Terrible hissing roar - Loana sees giant sea turtle moving among rocks toward Tumak. - Blows conch shell horn as a signal. - Second girl relays signal with her conch shell.

   B. Ledge of cliff. Lookout hears sound and repeats signal. Pan down to cave and village of skin huts.
      1. Shell men with spears run toward shore.
      2. Loana hurls small stones at the giant turtle to try to attract its attention. Its position is very close to Tumak.
      3. Shell men with spears see Tumak and aid in attracting its attention.
         a. Tumak is almost crushed with one foot of the turtle.
      4. Big battle as shell men finally drive giant turtle back into sea.

      5. Carry unconcious Tumak back to their village
         Dissolve.

V. SHELL PEOPLES VILLAGE
   A. We see they have a clean and well organized society.
      1. They have a primative form of art.
      2. (Progress as in original outline.)

2

Mr. Harryhausen

HAMMER FILM PRODUCTIONS LTD,   Page 3.
"ONE MILLION YEARS B.C."
Revised Studio Shooting Schedule Contd: 26.11.65.

DAY & DATE:	SET DESCRIPTION AND SCENE NUMBERS:	D/N	STAGE:	CHARACTERS:
MONDAY DEC. 6th.	TRAVELLING MATTE:		2	
	548 Red Lava Area	D		LOANA ?
	819 (Fight)	D		LOANA, SAKANA, TUMAK,
	820,826,827.	D		SURA, AHOT, ROCK HUNTER.
	767 Brontasaurus seq:	D		AKHOBA,NUPONDI,TOHANA, ULLA, Rock People.
	838 Earthquake seq:	D		Rock People.
TUESDAY DEC. 7th.	TRAVELLING MATTE:		2	
	473,474. Tree Cavern	DAWN		LOANA, TUMAK.
	492,498,501,503,507, 510,515,529. } Triceratops	D		LOANA, TUMAK.
	482A. (Treadmill ?)	"		LOANA, TUMAK.
WEDNESDAY DEC. 8th.	TRAVELLING MATTE:		2	
	Pterdactyl (Kirby Wire)			
	681,684,685,690,696.	D		LOANA
	857. Earthquake			1st ROCK MAN
	344G. Tree.			Young Shell Girl
THURSDAY DEC. 9th.	INT: CREVASSE		2	
	496,499,502,504,506, 508,510A,514,516,521.	D		TUMAK, LOANA.
	EXT: CREVASSE IN ROCKS		2	
	847,872.	D		AHOT, SURA.
	EXT: SMALL CAVE IN ROCKS		2	
	844,862,870.	D		TUMAK, LOANA.
PICK-UPS:	EXT: CRATER: C.S. Tumak 163A.			
	EARTHQUAKE: Ulla 853.			
	PTERDACTYL: Loana 663			
	N.B. Scs: 137,139. Deleted.			
FRIDAY DEC. 10th.	EXT: PLATEAU PRE-LIGHT		3	TUMAK,LOANA,AKHOBA,
	Reduction Matte 606,623. D			SAKANA,NUPONDI,TOHANA, ULLA, 1st ROCK MAN,
	607,-614,616-621. Tumak Organises Tribe.			YOUNG ROCK HUNTER,
	605,615,622. Akhoba watches.			Rock Hunters, Old Men, Women, Children.

SATURDAY/SUNDAY

3

FIRST TEST SLATE 1,000,000 YEARS. B.C. HAMMER

RAY HARRYHAUSEN

DATE 6th Dec. 1965.

Lighting -
Top Right   KEY   1   500 ft candles   750 wt Pup
Top Left Rear   FILLER   50 "   100 wt Inky
Level Left   FILLER   75 "   500 wt Pup
Floor off right } UNDER FILLER 50 "   100 wt Inky
of centre
Projector Reostat   N° 9   500 wt.

Centre of glass   220 f.c.   750 wt Pup

Fri

1,000,000 B.C.   HAMMER

RAY HARRYHAUSEN

Date. 1st July. 1966.   f.14. 170° Shutter
                                   filters 30 Magenta + 10 R + H/Glass
Scene   Take
   487   1

Lighting   F/C/P   Type
Top Left   KEY   850   750 wt Pup
Level Right   FILLER   270   500 " "
Forward Overhead   "   50 (with 51B   100 - Dink
                            Filter 4C)

Projector - Reostat Full - Lens 9 inch - Lamp 750 wt
   - B/P picture size approx 21 ins X 16 ins
   - Filters - 30 Magenta - 10 Red - Heat Glass in pro and
   ½ Kodak Blue with - N/D .3 + Steel Blue suspended
   for sky.

Camera - Lens - 100 mm

Scene - The first appearance of Ceratosaurus over
   brow of hill.

Note - Filter produced Red & Blue sky but processing produced
   pale blue & pale peach. (close shot)

1 A page from the Revised Outline dated 21 May 1965, which includes details of the original idea for the archelon sequence.

2 Page 3 from the travelling matte shooting schedule at Elstree Studios, dated 20 November 1965, for the first week of December. It was during this part of the shoot that Ray contracted pneumonia after rushing from his animation studio through icy weather to oversee the studio live-action plates.

3 A page from Ray's animation log. It is dated 6 December 1965 and is the first test slate.

4 Another page from his log. This is dated 1 July 1966, the last day of animation, and was for scene 487, the first appearance of the ceratosaurus.

5 Ray in his tiny Elstree studio holding up the allosaurus model. This was probably taken towards the end of the animation photography.

6 A photograph taken when the film was made, showing some of the models. Left to right: the allosaurus, the ceratosaurus, the brontosaurus (behind) and the triceratops.

The Valley of Gwangi (1969)

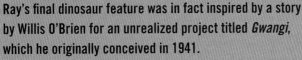

Ray's final dinosaur feature was in fact inspired by a story by Willis O'Brien for an unrealized project titled *Gwangi*, which he originally conceived in 1941.

During the making of *Mighty Joe Young*, O'Brien gave Ray a copy of his script and storyboards for the film. They told the story of a valley of dinosaurs ruled over by an allosaurus named Gwangi (a Native American word meaning lizard). Ray showed them to his producer Charles Schneer, who thought the concept was exciting and commissioned a new screenplay based on the original.

Originally called *The Valley Where Time Stood Still*, the film was set south of the Rio Grande at the turn of the twentieth century. In addition to Gwangi it featured an eohippus, a pterodactyl, an ornithomimus and a styracosaurus.

Ray did keep one major element in the story from O'Brien's version: a scene in which Gwangi is roped by cowboys. Even today, many years after Ray designed and animated this very complicated sequence, it is seen as one of the very best Ray Harryhausen scenes.

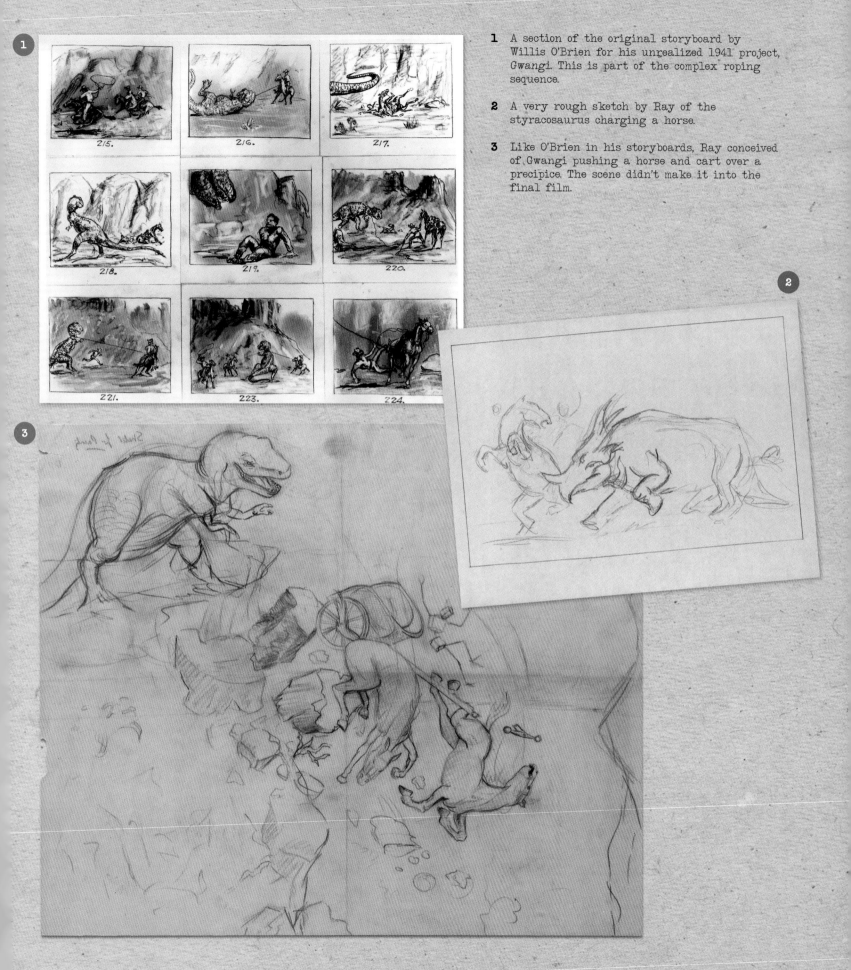

1 A section of the original storyboard by Willis O'Brien for his unrealized 1941 project, *Gwangi*. This is part of the complex roping sequence.

2 A very rough sketch by Ray of the styracosaurus charging a horse.

3 Like O'Brien in his storyboards, Ray conceived of Gwangi pushing a horse and cart over a precipice. The scene didn't make it into the final film.

1-6 Ray's key drawings for some of the major scenes in the film.

1 The Forbidden Valley was based on the strange rock formations in Ciudad Encantada in Spain, where the valley scenes were eventually filmed.

2 The pterodactyl snatches the boy from the horse.

3 The appearance of the tiny eohippus, which was accompanied on the soundtrack by the sound of a music box.

4 In the key drawing of Gwangi in the arena, the elephant attacks the cage in which Gwangi is kept.

In the film, Gwangi escapes from the cage first and then fights the elephant. The figure sitting in the bottom right with hands raised was posed by Diana, Ray's wife.

5 The fight between Gwangi and the styracosaurus, in which a rider spears the poor unsuspecting styracosaurus.

6 The roping of Gwangi. There is so much action in this rendition of Gwangi on the ground, struggling to get up.

MED. LONG. SHOT: GWANGI (Dyn) [391-393]
Gwangi pulls back as Tuck drops to
ground. Carlos ropes Gwangi pulling
his head back and aside.

MED. CLOSE SHOT: CARLOS [392]
As his rope gets taut. His horse
pulls back. Finally the rope snaps
off Gwangi's head.

CLOSE SHOT: -GWANGI- (Dyn) [393A]
He shakes the rope off. It falls
to the ground o.s.

MED. LONG SHOT:-GWANGI (Dyn) [393C]
He shakes rope loose. Tuck mounts
Carlos's horse and rides back toward
Gwangi. He turns from Carlos & goes
for Tuck.

MED. LONG: (Dyn) Tuck rides [395]
hard toward ledge as Champ and boys
ride in and rein up at sight of
Gwangi.

ROWDY turns abruptly [395 cont]
charging out rt. swinging his
rope. Gwangi goes after him as
others spread out.

CLOSE SHOT: TUCK as he swings [395B]
his rope, charging into camera.
He lets it fly o.s.

MED. LONG SHOT: (Dyn) [395C]
Tuck lets fly his lasso, roping
Gwangi's leg. He turns turtle,
rolling on his back.

Close Shot: (Dyn) GWANGI [395D]
As he thrashes about on the
ground.

Full Shot: (Dyn) GWANGI is [397]
down. T.J. swings her rope, lets
fly but misses his head. Bean rides in
lassos Gwangi's head pulling back.

Close Shot: Bean throwing his [397A]
lasso and pulling back. T.J.
in b.g. recoils for another throw.

Med. Long Shot: (Dyn) [397B]
Tuck pulls hard on Gwangi's foot.
The rope slips off. Gwangi starts
to get up.

Med. Long Shot: (Dyn)Gwangi [397D]
has regained his footing. His tail
snaps wildly.

Close Shot: TUCK as his [397C]
horse almost looses its balance
from the slipping of the rope.

Med. Close Shot: (Dyn) About [398]
to throw, Rowdy and his horse
are swept over by Gwangi's tail.

Full Shot: (Dyn) Rowdys [399]
horse scrambles to its feet
running off as Gwangi bears down on
Rowdy.

Close Shot:(Dyn) As Gwangi [399A]
goes after Rowdy. Rowdy backs
away in panic.

Full Shot: (Dyn) Gwangi goes [400]
after Rowdy. Champ rides in, leans
to the ground and snatches up rope
end. Does a flying mount and rides out.

Close Shot: ROWDY. We pan [400A]
with him as he scrambles back
in panic.

Full Shot: (Dyn)Champ pulls [401]
back jerking Gwangi's head up. Rowdy
runs for his horse.

Close Shot: TUCK he lets [401A]
his lasso fly o.s. It catches
Gwangi's head.

Long Shot: (Dyn) TUCKS [401B]
rope loops over Gwangi's head.
Champ pulls in opposite direction.

Close Shot: (Dyn) GWANGI [402A]
As he struggles to free himself
from the ropes.

Close Shot: Bean. He [402B]
throws his lasso, quickly
pulling back. Our view moves with
him.

1-3 Three pages of storyboards for the roping sequence. Again each
action is detailed by Ray to enable him to plan the live action as
well as the animation. This sequence was one of the most complex
in Ray's career and is certainly one of the most cinematically
exciting.

4 Seven tests done by Ray before the photography of the live action in Spain and before the models for the film were made. The models he used here are from *One Million Years B.C.* (the ceratosaurus, pteranodon and triceratops). They were reused in conjunction with cardboard cut-outs of the humans and horses that would make up key sequences.

1-2 Two more test frames using the triceratops and ceratosaurus from Ray's previous film.

3 A rare image of Gwangi during the roping sequence. Taken from a test after the split-screen process, all the live action is on the rear-projection screen and Gwangi is standing on the animation table, part of which can be seen on the right of the screen which is just above the matte line. When Ray filmed such scenes, he always focused on the rear screen rather than the model. This allowed the creature to be slightly soft and so match the rear-screen images.

4 Ray with Gila Golan, who played TJ, during the location photography in Ciudad Encantada, Spain.

5 Ray with the dreadful full-scale model of the pterodactyl. Ray always thought this, along with the full-size model of Gwangi, looked fake. The prop was used for the close-ups of the cowboy killing the creature.

6 The crew on location in the bullring in Almeria, Spain. Ray can be seen on the platform wearing his panama hat.

7 The director, James O'Connolly.

8 The cameraman Erwin Hillier in the Almeria bullring. Behind the cameras and Hillier sits Ray, wearing sunglasses.

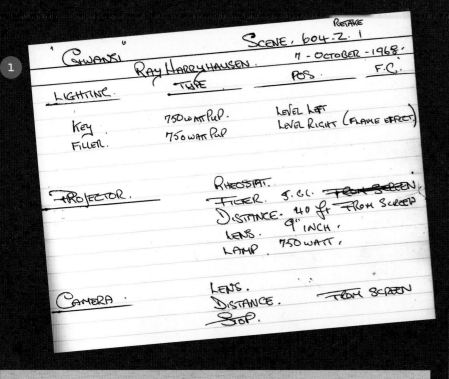

Handwritten animation log:

"Gwangi"   SCENE. 604·2. 1   RETAKE

Ray Harryhausen   TYPE   POS.   F.C.   7 · OCTOBER · 1968 ·

LIGHTING.

Key.   750 WATT PUP.   LEVEL LEFT
Filler.   750 WATT PUP   LEVEL RIGHT (FLAME EFFECT)

PROJECTOR.   RHEOSTAT.
               FILTER. J. G.L. ~~FROM SCREEN~~
               DISTANCE. 40 ft FROM SCREEN
               LENS. 9" INCH.
               LAMP. 750 WATT.

CAMERA.   LENS.
               DISTANCE.   FROM SCREEN
               STOP.

1 A page from Ray's animation log. It is dated 7 October 1968 and records scene 604–2.

2 The slate for the appearance of Gwangi and the lower matted-out area.

3 The composite shot of Gwangi looking at the riders.

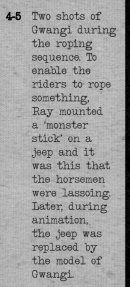

4-5 Two shots of Gwangi during the roping sequence. To enable the riders to rope something, Ray mounted a 'monster stick' on a jeep and it was this that the horsemen were lassoing. Later, during animation, the jeep was replaced by the model of Gwangi.

6 Gwangi fighting the styracosaurus.

7 The tiny eohippus trying to escape.

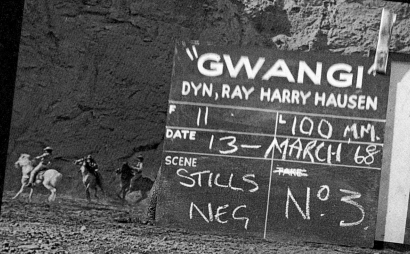

"GWANGI"
DYN. RAY HARRY HAUSEN
F 11   L 100 M.M.
DATE 13 – MARCH 68
SCENE   TAKE
STILLS
NEG   N°3.

8 A strip of 35mm test frames of the animation of the pterodactyl attacking the horsemen. The top of the rear-projection screen is visible. In front of this, suspended by aerial wires, is the model pterodactyl.

9-10 Two frames from the animation of the fight between Gwangi and the styracosaurus. The slate tells it all.

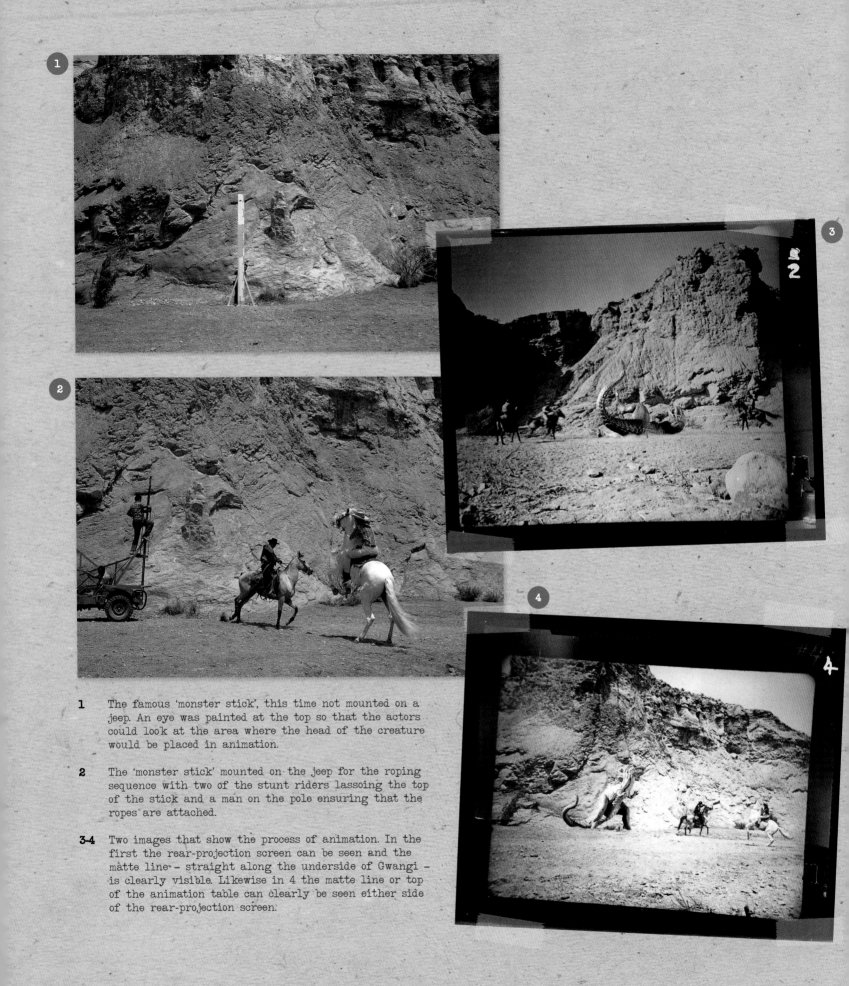

1 The famous 'monster stick', this time not mounted on a jeep. An eye was painted at the top so that the actors could look at the area where the head of the creature would be placed in animation.

2 The 'monster stick' mounted on the jeep for the roping sequence with two of the stunt riders lassoing the top of the stick and a man on the pole ensuring that the ropes are attached.

3-4 Two images that show the process of animation. In the first the rear-projection screen can be seen and the matte line – straight along the underside of Gwangi – is clearly visible. Likewise in 4 the matte line or top of the animation table can clearly be seen either side of the rear-projection screen.

a Charles H. Schneer production

THE VALLEY- WHERE TIME STOOD STILL

5 Ray in the stands of the Almeria bullring, probably trying to decide on the solution to a problem.

6 The crew again in the Almeria bullring.

7 This is the only piece of artwork we know of that shows the original title of the film. It is from an envelope printed before pre-production began.

8 A letter from the film's star, James Franciscus, to Charles Schneer opposing the change of name from *The Valley Where Time Stood Still* to *Gwangi* or *The Valley of Gwangi* as it would become known.

8

CABLE ADDRESS: CENTFOX, LOS ANGELES
TELEX & WESTERN UNION: 6-74875

Twentieth Century-Fox Television

BOX 900
BEVERLY HILLS, CALIFORNIA 90213

PHONE: (213) 277-2211

January 29, 1969

Mr. Charles Schneer
Amaran Films Ltd.
Suite One
13, Wigmore Street
London, W.1
ENGLAND

Dear Charlie:

It was nice talking to you yesterday, and I appreciate all of your understanding concerned with my feelings to retain the title THE VALLEY WHERE TIME STOOD STILL.

I am opposed to the title GWANGI for numerous reasons. Not the least of which is the sensational aspects the name itself contains.

Thank you so much for your understanding in this matter.

Best regards,

Jim

JAMES FRANCISCUS

JF:pi

cc Lederer
Anzarut
Hyman

A DIVISION OF TWENTIETH CENTURY-FOX FILM CORPORATION

Chapter 3

To Venus and Back

Whilst Ray is well known for his prehistoric and mythical subjects there is another genre that threads its way through his work: science fiction. He has always been a fan of classic science fiction writers such as Jules Verne and H.G. Wells, and made two excellent film adaptations of their novels –*Mysterious Island* and *First Men in the Moon*. Ray has also had a lifelong friendship with science fiction author Ray Bradbury, and the two made a childhood promise that they would one day work together. Regrettably, they never have. *The Beast From 20,000 Fathoms* was based on a Bradbury short story but the two men never collaborated on the project.

War of the Worlds (1949)

One of Ray's greatest regrets was not being able to gain enough interest from producers in making a film of H.G. Wells' novel *War of the Worlds*. He considered the plotline as very suitable for stop-motion and touted the idea, storyboards and key drawings all over Hollywood in an effort to stimulate interest. The response was always that it wasn't commercial, which shows that sometimes producers need to have vision because George Pal's live-action 1953 version was a box office hit. Ray's version went through many metamorphoses, being first set in Victorian times in the southern counties of England, then in modern-day America. However what he did manage to reproduce in his artwork from the original story were Wells' tentacled Martians, and their war machines, tripod structures that spit a destructive ray. Ray built a Martian and photographed around 4 minutes of colour test footage of the creature emerging from the spacecraft, but even that wasn't enough to convince the producers.

1

1 A key drawing of the hero being attacked by a Martian in the cellar sequence.

2-3 Three very early concepts for Wells' Martian as described in the novel, which include the huge head and tentacles. The facial features were altered for the final model.

4 A description, typed by Ray, of Wells' Martian, on which he based his design.

THE MARTIAN

The martian is a truly amazing being.   An entitie without wisdom but with a tremendous over developed intelligence.

I would like to try to account for its strange and rather overbering physiognomy. In contrast to the human being, the martian being has one part head to two parts body. The Human being it is well known, is porportioned as one part head to six part body.

This impressive increase in brain cavity has caused the less functional parts of its body to diminish considerabbly and in some cases completely disappear. The body for example , contains a tremendous number of organs and requires a great degree of nourishment in the human race. In the martian race this superfulus bulk has been modified and condensed to such a degree that it no longer noticably exists. The heart it seems has been neatly tucked away into what may be termed, the neck of the thing. The lungs too have been reduced in size and shape taking their place just below the medula of the brain.

The martian's appendages have been increased and made similar in sie and shape radiating in all directions from the base of the bulky neck.   There are six in number and measure about eight feet in length. These , shall we say arms, are cilindrical in shape tapering off in diameter to a greatly modified hand. An amazing amount of strength and flexibility is obtained in this rather unigue structure.   The modified hand I spoke of consists of only two fingers which I might parralel with the human hand of the index finger and thumb.   Actually when one stops and c considers the structure of the hand we find that the fingers I mentioned are used nine tenths of the times particularly for the more intricate actions.

I spoke earlier of the Martians keen intellect. What could be more conceivably horrible than an intellectual being lacking wisdom.   In the human race, and I believe it can be said of the martians, there is a great difference between intellect and wisdom.   It is ironical that intellect can exist wthout wisdom but wisdom cannot exist without intellect.

1

By the toll of a billion deaths man has
bought his birthright of the earth, and it is
his against all comers. For neither do men
life nor die in vain.   --Worlds Greatest Books
(War of the Worlds
P.P. 133)

3

Ideas for sequences (War of the Worlds)

1 Introduce through proper motivation
a scene of a boy prodding an
ant hill with a stick which will
be the cause of discussion & comparison
of the invaders from Mars.

2

①

1. The brutalities of the human race towards
man + animals.

2. The self-satisfaction of the human
race... the vain belief that they are the
only intelligent form of life anywhere.

3. The self centered person who tries to
outdo everyone with whom he comes in
to contact with.

4. Various shots of the way people waste their
time + life. Emphasize this point.

SUGGESTIONS FOR SKETCHES
(War of the Worlds)

1.   Men looking at a rocket, suggesting a falling star.

2.   An enormous hole had been made by the impact of the
projectile, and the sand and gravel had been flung
violently in every direction over the heath and
heather, forming heaps visible a mile and a half
away.   The heather was on fire eastward, and a
thin blue smoke rose against the dawn.

3.   The cylinder had a diameter of about thirty yards.
Cylinder is very hot. Man looks on in amazement.

4.   The crowd about the pit had increased and stood
out black against the lemon-yellow of the sky- a
couple of hundred people, perhaps.

5.   The end of the cylinder was being screwed out from
within. Nearly two feet of shining screw projected.
Somebody blundered against me, and I narrowly missed
being pitched on to the top of the screw.   I turned
and as I did so the screw must have come out, and
the lid of the cylinder fell upon the gravel with
a ringing concussion.

6.   Looking into the cylinder I presently saw something
stirring within the shadow; grayish billowy
movements, one above another, and then two luminous
disks-like eyes.   Then something resembling a
little gray snake, about the thickness of a walking
-stick, coiled up out of the writhing middle, and
wriggled in the air towards me-and then another.
A big grayish, rounded bulk, the size, perhaps, of
a bear, was rising slowly and painfully out of the
cylinder. As it bulged up and caught the light, it
glistened like wet leather.   Two large dark-
colored eyes were regarding me steadfastly,. It
was rounded, and had one might say, a face. There
was a mouth under the eyes, the lipless brim of
which quivered and panted, and dropped saliva.
The body heaved and pulsated convulsively.   A
lank tentacular appendage gripped the edge of the
cylinder, another swayed in the air.
The peculiar V shaped mouth with its pointed upper
lip, the absence of brow ridges, the absence of
a chin beneath the wedge-like lower lip, the incessant
quivering of this mouth, the Gorgon groups of tentacles, the
tumultuous breathing of the lungs in a strange atmosphere
the evident heaviness and painfulness of movement,
due to the greater gravitational energy of the earth--
above all the extraordinary intensity of the immense
eyes.

4

WAR OF THE WORLDS   .....Story suggestion..

The story takes place just at the close
of world war II.   Our hero is a very good
airplane pilot who has won countless metals
for his heroism.   Hence he is chosen by
a doctor who has invented a rocket space ship
its location being somewhere in Siberia.
The ship takes off for the moon and it journey
is very successfull.   We follow them to the
moon.   The group come across all sorts of
weird and fantastic monsters and finally return
to the earth.

5

WAR OF THE WORLDS

could have the opening in a hospital or some place
where doctors could perform an autopsy on one of
the martians.   we avoid showing the actual martian
but discuss it.   Doctor could be called out of the
laboratory by an newspaper reporter who would like to
have the story of a man who had close contact with
these creatures since the invasion from mars.   The
doctor could be our expository device with the scene
going back to several months earlier.   From there we
start at the observatory scene or various short sequences
showing humanity in general going about their own little
lives.///

6

Bridge scene

Show a great Bridge - Perhaps
the Brooklyn Bridge crowded
with people.
            Martian destroys bridge.
Shots of bridge collapsing & people
falling into the river.

Holland Tunnel for a location.

---

1   A moving quote, typed by Ray, from Wells' War of the Worlds, explaining how man has earned his right to live on planet Earth. This line greatly impressed Ray.

2-3   Ray's ideas for the overall theme of the film with emphasis on the beginning of the story and man's inhumanity towards other life on our planet. At this stage of his life, Ray would often type out a number of ideas and thoughts for projects.

4   A plot idea headed War of the Worlds, although it does read as if Ray was thinking of another storyline.

5   Another opening for the film, one in which doctors perform an autopsy on a Martian.

6   A handwritten idea for the destruction of the Brooklyn Bridge in New York.

7   A list of key drawings for the War of the Worlds project, dated 27 November 1942.

8 A sheet of sketches for the visualization of a tri-legged Martian vehicle.

9 A very atmospheric key drawing of Martian tripods stalking through a decimated town with people running before them. Someone pointed out that there are three crosses just under the machine off in the distance. This was not intentional; they are simply part of a ruined building.

10 Once Ray had begun to make key drawings he had also decided on what his Martians would look like, so in these rough sketches he has begun the process of designing the armatures.

11 An unfinished key drawing of the first Martian emerging from its capsule.

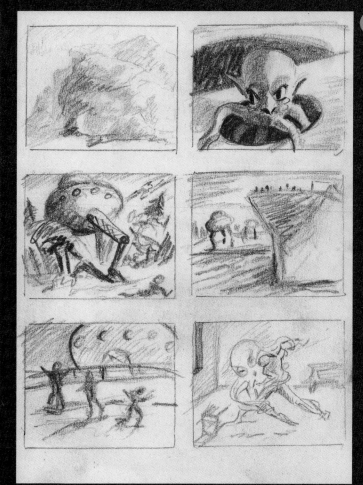

1 Part of an early rough storyboard featuring an observatory that follows the first capsule to leave Mars and crash on Earth.

2 A second early storyboard showing the Martian emerging from the capsule and the first tripod wreaking havoc.

3 An early charcoal and pencil sketch with highlights depicting the crashed capsule and people swarming around.

4 Another charcoal and pencil sketch with highlights for the unscrewing of the capsule door.

5-7 Three key images for the proposed project, all drawn in charcoal and pencil with highlights.

5 A man is hit by the death ray.

6 The first sight of the Martian tentacles as they emerge from the capsule.

7 A horse and cart are startled by a Martian tripod.

The Elementals (1952)

The idea of a creature being brought to earth in a spaceship was to be a recurring theme in Ray's early movies. In this original story, conceived by Ray, a scientist and his wife discover a crashed spacecraft in the Pyrenees Mountains and take a chrysalis they had found nearby back to their laboratory. What they call an Elemental (a bat-like creature) hatches, rapidly breeds and spreads across France. The story ends in a fiery climax in and around the Eiffel Tower and on the river Seine in Paris. Ray had always dreamed of travelling to Europe and so set the story specifically in France.

   To demonstrate what could be achieved by model stop-motion animation, Ray built a model of one Elemental and photographed himself being attacked and carried off in the creature's talons. Sadly, although he touted the project around many producers, including Jack Dietz, who had co-produced *The Beast From 20,000 Fathoms*, neither he nor anyone else was interested.

STORY IDEA   (Science fiction.)   2/20/53

An entomologist and his wife are searching for
~~hither to scaree specimins of insect in some~~
remote section of the world. Possibly Spain.
He comes across, in the forest, a huge chrysalis
fastened to a tree.   The thing is about eight
feet long and looks very much like a butterfly
chrysalis. Being a man of science he must
watch it develope and makes arrangements
to have it carefully ~~shipped~~ back to his lab or
work shop.   In this remote spot he also
finds many other such speciments. ~~Amhon~~

   Also finds what may resemble giant worms.
   They are dead and are lying scattered

((VARRIATION ON BAT MAN IDEA)

An archiologist and his group come across
a chrysalis hidden between some rocks in
a remote section (say Italy or Sicily) while
exploring some old ~~muhmamon~~ ancient ruins.

They remove Chrysalis and take it by truck,
to a near by friends house who has an old
barn that has been converted into an amateur
laboratory.   The friend is an entomologist
and has many specimins of bugs and rare
insects.   They house the giant chrysalis
in the barn.   They do not tell the news
papers or athorities for fear the find may
be taken away from them and thus die.

---

(2)
   of some strange race of man.
   The creature is belligerent and looks upon
the human race as just so many ants to get
rid of.   After a night of terror in the
doctors workshop the thing is overcome .
   It is shipped to Paris, or Madrid to a
medical association for further study.
   In the meantime it is remembered that there
are other chrysalis in the forest that must
be destroyed before they hatch.   When the
doctor arrives with an army of men the Chrysalis
are already open and the occupants gone.
   Nothing is heard of the creature for sometime

*Long height shot of doctor + men from Fire Zips
of their dash into smoke...*

The thing struggles for life as it imerges from
its shell like encasement.   .

Many more such chrysaliss have been found and
our scientist compare or rather suggest that
this same thing has happened many years ago
and is actually the origin of Greek Mythology.
Particularly they idea of the gians and Cyclops.

There is an invasion of a city by the giants
 and our story shows varios episods of
   the attempted distruction as the ruthless
 savage giants try to destroy our civilization.
They even fight among themselves.

1 Four cards, dated 20 February
   1953, detailing story ideas for
   The Elementals.

2 A very rough sketch of one
   of the bat-like creatures,
   called an Elemental, clinging
   to a spire in Paris, possibly
   belonging to the Cathédrale
   Notre Dame de Paris.

Feb. 20. 1953

(Outline for a screen story)

THE ELEMENTALS
by
Ray Harryhausen

An entomologist and his wife are searching for a hither-to scarce specimen of insect believed to exist in a remote section of the Pyreneese mountains, France.   Accompanying the doctor and his wife is the doctors assistant and the doctors German police dog, Buck.

In pursuit of a specimen of rare butter-fly the entomologist, whom we will call doctor, sees a number of vultures circling in the air close by.   Buck gains the scent of something and runs off into the underbrush.   The doctor follows.   As he parts the bushes he discovers a semi-clearing with the earth thrust up all about forming a crater like hole.   The corpse of several enormous worms lie near the center are crushed pieces of metalic shell resembling the outer casing of a projectile near the rim of the crater.   Upon examination it is found that they are made of some sort.   The dead worms are enormous from a completely unknown alloy.   and are half eaten away by the birds and vultures but enough remains to give the impression of giant worms.

We see tracks of dried slime, much like the trail of a snail, leading in three directions from the pit and disappearing in the under-brush.

The doctor is joined by his wife and assistant.   They follow one of the trails of glistening slime.   We hear the barking of Buck up ahead.   Upon arrival our four principles are confronted by a grate Chrysalis fastened to a large tree.   The thing is about eight feet in length and resembles a butterfly chrysalis including its periodic, convulsive movements.   The gargantuan size of course astounds everyone.   The assistant wants to crack it open and see what is inside but the doctor insists on taking it back by truck to the farm house they have rented for the summer.   Being a man of science he must watch it develop.

There is a discovery made of twelve other Chrysalis, the same in shape and gigantic size.   The doctor sends for the truck and carefully cuts down the Chrysalis structure and loads it into the truck.   It is shipped back to the farm house.

The rare specimen is placed in the barn that has been converted into a tempory laboratory.   There are many specimen jars all about .   The new find is suspended in a position similar to its original position on the tree.   The doctor believes the thing may open within a day or two.   There is much speculation as to the reason for its enormous size and exactly what will emerge when it has matured.

Early in the morning, about 3 A.M. the doctor's wife is awakened by a crackling noise coming from inside the barn.   The doctor, his dog, wife and assistant enter the barn in time to see the final phase of the metemorphis of the chrysalis.

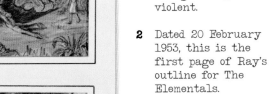

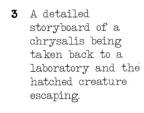

1 An Elemental clutching a human in its talons, whilst at the same time pulling a woman off the Eiffel Tower by her hair. When Ray saw this again after many years he thought it quite violent.

2 Dated 20 February 1953, this is the first page of Ray's outline for The Elementals.

3 A detailed storyboard of a chrysalis being taken back to a laboratory and the hatched creature escaping.

4 A key drawing (the only one) of a pilot faced with a group of Elementals, one carrying a helpless woman, flying towards him.

5 A colour test from the few minutes of footage Ray shot of himself trying to scare the creature away. At the end of the test, the creature catches Ray (who turns into a small model) and flies away. One of the wires supporting the model can be seen behind it on the far right.

It Came From Beneath the Sea (1955)

Following the success of *The Beast From 20,000 Fathoms*, Ray was introduced to a young producer at Columbia named Charles H. Schneer, who wanted to make a picture about a giant octopus that terrorizes San Fransisco. This was the start of a business association and friendship that would last for almost thirty years. The film was produced by Charles for the Sam Katzman unit at Columbia Pictures. Ray remembers showing Katzman and Charles his designs for the giant octopus and being told by the former that it looked nothing like one. Ray was shocked as he had been studying the creatures in detail, but soon realized that Katzman's idea of a cephalopod was based on the octopus in *Popeye*, and was hardly accurate. In the end Ray was able to build a realistic model of the creature, but to save costs he gave it only six tentacles, making it a sixtopus!

MONSTER BENEATH THE SEA

STEP OUTLINE

OF NEW ENDING

by

George Worthing Yates

This begins at the present scene 136, p. 88, of the
script. It presumes that in the scene with the newspapermen (sc. 175,
p. 90) the map of San Francisco bay area has been established
and the two separate bridges definitely planted to prevent
confusion between them.

Continuity-wise, this is preceded by scenes that convey
the public has been made aware of the giant octopus, and measures
being taken to protect San Francisco and other West Coast cities
from it. In line with making the reaction of the public as
factual as possible, it will be suggested that people as yet
show no sign of fear, only curiosity and in some cases, disbelief.

GGGGGGGGGGG

EXT. OCEAN - DAY

FULL SHOT, RUNNING, FROM GOLDEN GATE BRIDGE
Again the sea is empty. This is a SHOT FROM POV of a
car crossing the bridge.

EXT. GOLDEN GATE BRIDGE - DAY

MEDIUM PAN SHOT, REVERSE ANGLE, ON CAR CROSSING BRIDGE
The people in it are staring out to sea as it drives
slowly past. Other cars in SHOT also contain sightseers,
in no hurry to get across.

FULL SHOT OF BRIDGE
This shows the bridge fairly full of traffic, travelling
at moderate speed, and detouring to make way around Navy
trucks and personnel parked in the middle of the span, and
partly blocking the Southbound lanes.

MEDIUM SHOT NAVY TECHNICIANS AT SONAR TRUCK
Dialogue will convey that these men are in touch with

CONTINUED:

---

1 The first page of the original step outline by George
Worthing Yates for the new ending for *Monster Beneath
the Sea*, which became *It Came From Beneath the Sea*.

2 Dated 16 December 1953, this is the first page of a
memo from Steve Fisher at Columbia Pictures about the
special effects needed for the proposed opening scene: the
submarine's first encounter with the giant octopus. At
this stage the production is called *Monster of the Deep*.

From: Steve Fisher

Dec. 16, 1953

MONSTER OF THE DEEP
(Prod. #8260)

Proposed, tentative need for the
following Special Effects,
Miniatures, etc.

1. The "monster" itself, a giant octopus. Audience should get
the impression it is so big that each of the tentacles are
about a thousand feet long; all other details proportionate.
Other than size, the beast is no different in description
from any other octopus. It is capable of discharging tons
of inky substance that can blacken a whole harbor.

2. Atomic submarine. For description, see COLLIERS magazine
attached hereto. (Return to author, please, when finished
with it.)

3. Undersea cavern, bleak, barren, quite dark.

4. Submarine encounters octopus in cavern, in outright collision
with the "ball" of the beast when it makes a sudden move.
Intense struggle of octopus to destroy submarine. The sub
continually slithers out from the suction cups of the giant
tentacles. Sub torpedoes monster, but torpedoes are without
warheads (carried only in time of actual war) and they do not
even penetrate the body of the octopus, instead are dented,
twisted.

Considerable damage to sub, outside and in. Inside sub,
showing water three or four feet deep, leaks, damage to
structure. (This cannot be miniature, as actors must work
in the scenes.)

Sea inside cavern blackened by inky substance, total darkness.

5. Sub limps to Manila for repairs.

6. Sub skipper flies to Washington, D.C. from Manila.

7. Giant octopus now out of cavern, in open sea. Naval craft
trying to chart its movement. A destroyer is come upon by
the beast. A giant tentacle wraps around it, drawing it under
the water, crushing it. It cannot escape like the sub for
once it is under the surface it is lost; the sub could still
navigate after being seized by the long black arm of the
beast.

8. Navy mine sweep attacked by beast. In this shot, two or
more of the tentacles lift the craft out of the ocean and high
into the air, seven hundred feet high, with the terrified
crew still aboard. Then the ship is crashed into the ocean,
and all are lost.

3 A series of rough
sketches drawn by Ray
whilst discussing the
creature at Columbia
Pictures with Charles
Schneer and Sam
Katzman. Katzman
wanted the octopus sac
to be upright, as he had
seen in *Popeye* cartoons,
because he assumed that
was how they looked.
Ray took great care to
illustrate exactly how
a real octopus looked,
with the sac behind.

Helicopter Sequence

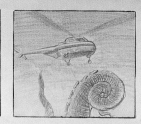

FORM 174-50 RMS 11-52

INTER-OFFICE **COLUMBIA** **COMMUNICATION**

To _Mr. Charles Schneer_   From _Ray Harryhausen_

Attention of _____   By _____

In Regard to _IT CAME FROM BENEATH THE SEA_ Date _November 5, 1954_

The following are the miniatures that were eliminated in the $5,500. budget cut before pre-production. Naturally this elimination would have an effect on the first estimate of the final footage of the picture:

1. Pylons .... break-away (above and beneath water).

2. Covered dock .... break-away.

3. Large scale section of break-away bridge for boat sequence. (PP #10).

4. Large scale section of break-away stern for boat sequence. (PP #8).

5. Three miniature cars for fall-off, San Francisco bridge.

Just before shooting, several other scenes were eliminated:

1. Front shot of man fleeing from tentacle.

2. Side shot of tentacle pursuing man across screen.

3. Up shot of tentacle coming down toward man.

4. Man falling from box car (two shots -- CU and MLS)

5. Down shot (PP #38) of car on bridge.

6. Raft scenes in boat sequence (two shots)

7. Bridge scene was trimmed.

Special Effects
"IT CAME FROM BENEATH THE SEA"
(Columbia)

The following outline lists the four major Special Effects sequences from the film as they will appear on the screen.

1. TRAMP STEAMER SEQUENCE: A giant octopus attacks a tramp steamer at sea. The ship is demolished and finally pulled beneath the waves.

    SPECIAL EFFECTS employed to achieve illusion;
    -Process photography-
    -Animated miniature model-
    -Miniature projection-
    -Double exposure-

2. GOLDEN GATE BRIDGE SEQUENCE: Aggravated by an electrical charge the giant octopus attacks and succeeds in destroying the San Francisco Golden Gate Bridge. After the destruction it slithers back into the bay waters.

    SPECIAL EFFECTS employed to achieve illusion;
    -Animated miniature model-
    -Process photography-
    -Matte and double exposure-
    -Miniature-
    -Miniature projection-

3. WATERFRONT AND CITY SEQUENCE: The San Francisco waterfront is menaced by the giant octopus. Its tentacles destroy the Embarcadero and Ferry Building. With the use of flame-throwers it is driven back into the sea.

    SPECIAL EFFECTS employed to achieve illusion;
    -Miniatures combined with real backgrounds-
    -Animated miniature model-
    -Traveling Matte-
    -Process photography-
    -Split screen-
    -Miniature projection-

4. UNDERWATER AND SUBMARINE SEQUENCE: A remote controlled torpedo is fired into the flesh of the octopus. The octopus clutches the submarine pinning it to the ocean floor. The commander of the submarine blasts the octopus' eye with an explosive so that the ship will be free of the hold that the octopus has taken. When the submarine is clear of the beast the remote controlled torpedo is exploded. The giant octopus is blasted to bits.

    SPECIAL EFFECTS employed to achieve illusions;
    -Process photography-
    -Traveling matte-
    -Animated miniature model-
    -Miniature projection-

---

1 A storyboard for an unrealized helicopter sequence.

2 Another unrealized scene – a proposed first encounter between the submarine and the octopus in an underwater abyss that was to have taken place at the start of the film.

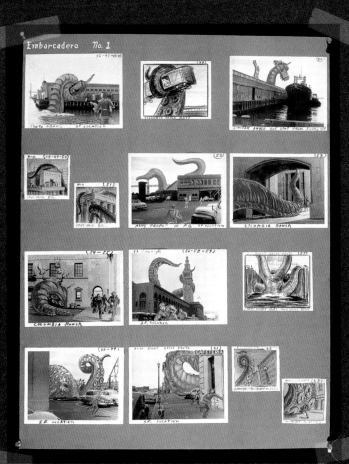

Embarcadero No. 1

3 The original miniature submarine and torpedo that appear at the end of the film in the underwater sequence in San Francisco harbour. Both are made from wood by Ray.

4 An inter-office Columbia Pictures memo dated 5 November 1954, from Ray to Charles Schneer, concerning the $5,500 exclusion of various miniatures and animation shots before pre-production.

5 A memo from Ray about the final special effects sequences required for the film.

6 A storyboard sequence of the octopus attacking the Embarcadero and the Ferrygate in San Francisco. Most of it is sketched on photographs of the locations with a few simple sketches to illustrate the action.

7-8 The octopus attacking the Embarcadero. Two tentacles are threatening the tower, readying to pull it down. In image 7 the tower is real and is part of the split-screen matted-out area seen in image 8.

9 A rare shot of two of the large tentacles (these were separate models from the six-tentacled model) beginning to wrap around the model of the tower on the animation table.

10 Another very rare shot, showing the full armatured octopus model lying on the miniature bed of San Francisco harbour. Ray used a distortion glass to simulate water for the scene.

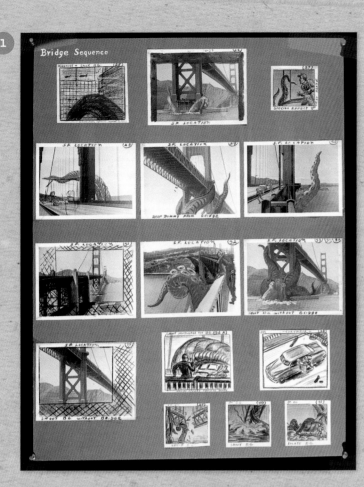

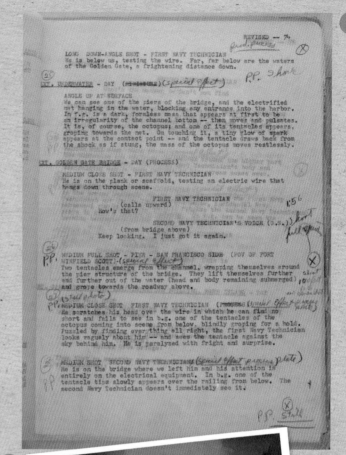

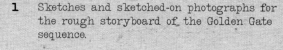

1   Sketches and sketched-on photographs for the rough storyboard of the Golden Gate sequence.

2   Page 74 of the revised screenplay that includes part of the Golden Gate sequence, with Ray's notes.

3-4   A split-screen shot, with 3 showing the matted out lower section and 4 the final combined image.

5   A set-up in Ray's animation studio in which three large tentacles destroy the bridge. These seperate tentacles were recently found in the LA garage although most of the latex had fallen away, leaving the armatures exposed.

6   Ray filming a slightly different Golden Gate scene. This time the large tentacles are crushing the bridge support.

7   A rare test image of the octopus at sea, with the miniature submarine in its tentacles. This sequence was never used and until recently we didn't know that Ray had shot such a test.

8   Another rare image showing the armatured octopus model dragging the boat down. The two rods on the underside of the model boat allowed Ray to rock the models up and down a frame at a time.

9   One of the large tentacles being animated against the rear-projection screen. On the right can be seen the matted-out glass for the spilt-screen process.

Earth vs. The Flying Saucers (1956)

It was Charles Schneer's idea to make a film that exploited the then current craze for flying saucers. The screenplay was based on a best-selling book called *Flying Saucers From Outer Space* by Donald Keyhoe, about reported UFO sightings. The only animation in the picture is the saucers themselves and collapsing buildings. There was no budget for high-speed photography of the miniatures of the crumbling Washington landmarks, so Ray had to attach all the miniature columns, bricks and stonework to wires and animate them separately. He designed the saucer models with upper and lower fluted areas, which were animated, and suspended each of the models on three wires, each of which had to be painted the same colour as the background live-action plate.

1 A charcoal and pencil sketch for aliens appearing in the desert, a scene that was never filmed.

2 A schedule of dates, dated 13 May 1955, for the completion of *Attack of the Flying Saucers*, the original name for the film. It is an incredibly tight schedule and Ray had only three days to carry out the initial recce in Washington. He later went back to take photographs for the cinematographer.

3 The first sketch design for the flying saucer standing on its landing plinth.

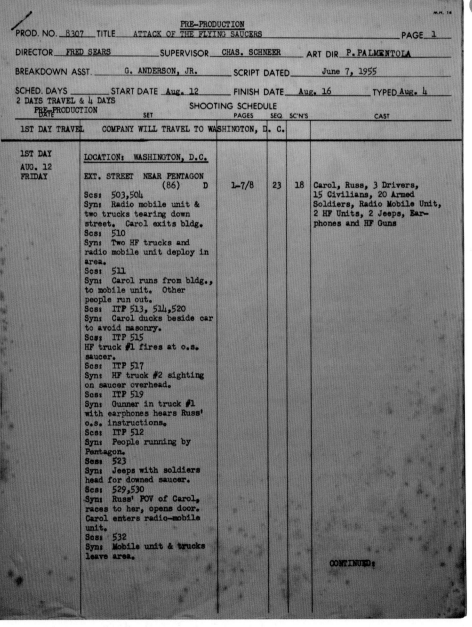

1-2 Two more quick sketches by Ray of a desert sequence in which a soldier is confronted by the aliens and killed by the death ray.

3 A sketch on photographic paper of saucers attacking or crashing into the Capitol Building.

4 Part of the live-action shooting schedule dated 4 August 1955. It suggests that the number of days scheduled were '2 days' travel and 4 days' pre-production'. Even for Sam Katzman's unit, this was a remarkably tight turnaround.

PRE-PRODUCTION

M.M. 14

PROD. NO. 8307   TITLE   ATTACK OF THE FLYING SAUCERS   PAGE 1

DIRECTOR FRED SEARS _____ SUPERVISOR CHAS. SCHNEER ___ ART DIR P. PALMENTOLA

BREAKDOWN ASST. _____ G. ANDERSON, JR. _____ SCRIPT DATED _____ June 7, 1955

SCHED. DAYS _____ START DATE Aug. 12 _____ FINISH DATE ___ Aug. 16 _____ TYPED Aug. 4
2 DAYS TRAVEL & 4 DAYS
PRE-PRODUCTION   SHOOTING SCHEDULE

DATE	SET	PAGES	SEQ.	SC'N'S	CAST
1ST DAY TRAVEL	COMPANY WILL TRAVEL TO WASHINGTON, D. C.				
1ST DAY AUG. 12 FRIDAY	LOCATION: WASHINGTON, D.C. EXT. STREET NEAR PENTAGON (86) D Scs: 503,504 Syn: Radio mobile unit & two trucks tearing down street. Carol exits bldg. Scs: 510 Syn: Two HF trucks and radio mobile unit deploy in area. Scs: 511 Syn: Carol runs from bldg., to mobile unit. Other people run out. Scs: ITP 513, 514,520 Syn: Carol ducks beside car to avoid masonry. Scs: ITP 515 HF truck #1 fires at o.s. saucer. Scs: ITP 517 Syn: HF truck #2 sighting on saucer overhead. Scs: ITP 519 Syn: Gunner in truck #1 with earphones hears Russ' o.s. instructions. Scs: ITP 512 Syn: People running by Pentagon. Scs: 523 Syn: Jeeps with soldiers head for downed saucer. Scs: 529,530 Syn: Russ' POV of Carol, races to her, opens door. Carol enters radio-mobile unit. Scs: 532 Syn: Mobile unit & trucks leave area.	1-7/8	23	18	Carol, Russ, 3 Drivers, 15 Civilians, 20 Armed Soldiers, Radio Mobile Unit, 2 HF Units, 2 Jeeps, Ear-phones and HF Guns
					CONTINUED:

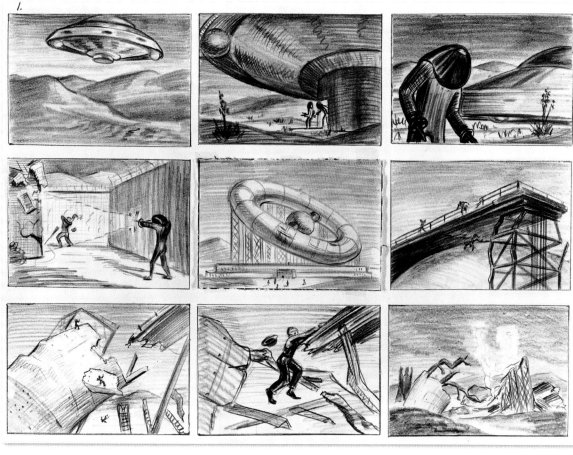

5-6 Two pages of
storyboards by
Ray showing
the destruction
of the Skyhook
research centre
by saucers
and various
encounters with
saucers. Most
of these scenes
appeared in the
final film.

#4

Sc. 210   Sc. 211-213

Sc. 215-220-222   Sc. 223   Sc. 223 cont.-227-229   Sc. 225   (Process)

1 The encounter with the saucer on the beach. The beach is actually Point Dume, north of Malibu, where Ray had bought a plot of land for a planned house. The pictures again use photographs and sketches to show the action.

2 A list of stock shots needed for rear-projection plates. They would have been supplied by the film library at Columbia.

3 Ray's list of miniature sets required for the production, which total just over $5000.

1.

ATTACK OF THE FLYING SAUCERS

H-PROCESS PLATES

1. **Sc. 3**   JET COCKPIT DAY Through plastic bubble we see saucer up ahead. Sound effect as pilot throttles up for maximum power for chase.

2. **Sc. 5**   JET COCKPIT DAY as saucer disappears.

3. **Sc. 14**   TRANSCONTINENTAL PLANE COCKPIT DAY Pilot's POV. Saucer appears to be bearing down on them with tremendous speed. Pilot makes a motion which puts plane into dive.

4. **Sc. 16**   Int. TRANSCONTINENTAL PLANE CABIN Passengers POV. A saucer can be seen quite distinctly as it maneuvers past window of plane then streaks away at great speed.

5. **Sc. 35**   INT. CAR DAY   Carol and Russ in the f.g. Between them, through the rear window, can be seen the retreating roadway. An enormous circular object dips into scene and appears to be overtaking the car.

6. **Sc. 36**   INT. CAR DAY SHOOTING THROUGH THE windshield of the car. The backs of Carol and Russ frame the f.g. The saucer swoops down over the road ahead of them and moves ahead at a majestic speed.

8. **Sc. 38**   SAME AS 36 Carol steps on the gas and drives ahead at full speed. The saucer easily outspeeds them, increasing the distance between it and the car until it is about a quarter of a mile ahead of them. .... It floats easily for a moment then with startling suddenness it reverses direction and comes back at the car with incredible speed. The full looming shape of the saucer fills the space visible through the windshield. It looks as though it is about to crash into the car.

9. **Sc. 68**   MEDIUM CLOSE SHOT UP-ANGLE HOUSE IN B.G. NIGHT Harrison looks up and the other two follow the direction of his gaze. Two small, round, fuzzy lights that look like a photograph of a total eclipse of the sun with a very black round center and a wavering corona-like effect around the rim float in the sky in b.g. The light is no sooner seen than it disappears.

10. **Sc. 91** INT. OBSERVATION TOWER DAY Nash and Harrison stare out the windows of the observation tower. through which they see an enormous saucer approaching to within one hundred yards of the tower, its two halves spinning in opposite directions. It moves forward, gliding majestically over the heads of the observers.

11. **Sc. 131** MEDIUM LONG SHOT JEEP AND BUILDING. Eminations enter scene building explodes.

12. **Sc. 142** INT. DOME OF SAUCER Framed in the f.g. can be seen the head, hand, and shoulder of Harrison resting on his elbows. In the b.g. can be seen the corrugated dome of the saucer. The dome moves closer, giving the effect Harrison and camera are on the interior of the retracting stem. Harrison turns his head to look up.

13. **Sc. 144** INT. OF SAUCER Harrison in the f.g. stands up from "one-kneeposition," observing his surroundings. In b.g. we see the glistening corrugated metallic walls of the saucer. In one segment a wide, rectangular flat metal partition like a fin (8 feet by 10 feet) breaks from the wall at a 30 degree angle, which later proves to be a television screen.

MINIATURES

1. Capital Dome
2. Washington Monument
3. Justice building
4. Street corner and marquee   500
5. Up shot corner of building   400
6. Interior of Union station   800
7. ~~Interior wall of capitol.~~ capital steps.

4 The miniature set of the Supreme Court Building in Washington DC. The far columns and pediment are in the process of buckling and collapsing after an attack. Each miniature column and stone had to be animated to simulate a collapsing building, and this process was repeated with the models of the Washington Monument, the Capitol Building and Union Station.

5 The largest of the model saucers, suspended on its aerial brace by three wires, is about to crash into the Capitol Building. On the left-hand side of the animation table is a miniature of that section of the building into which the saucer is to crash, and behind this is a large photograph of the rest of the building, including the dome.

6 The same sequence from another angle. Here the aerial brace is more prominent.

20 Million Miles to Earth (1957)

This is probably the closest Ray ever got to animating a version of *King Kong*. The creature, or Ymir, is brought back to Earth by a US space expedition to Venus. Much as Kong had been taken against his will to New York, the Ymir had been brought to Earth and so into an alien environment. Ray manages to instil such wonderful tragedy into his creation – a combination of dinosaur, human and fish – that at its demise the audience feels pathos, not relief. The idea was thought up by Ray, but with the help of Charlotte (sometimes spelled 'Charlott') Knight, a friend who had helped with his Fairy Tales. They wrote an outline called *The Cyclops*, set in and around Chicago, but this location was changed to Italy as Ray still wanted to get to Europe. The project was later retitled *The Giant Ymir* and then *20 Million Miles to Earth*.

1. Crash of Rocket ship
2. Retrieve one body & cylinder
3. Sinking of ship
4. coming of air force men
5. take creature back to San Diego
6. Doctor revives it & notices its growth
7.

1-2 Two early sketches for the Ymir. The body, arms and legs are as they will appear in the final model, but the head is too lizard-like.

3 Notes by Ray on early scenes for one of the first step outlines, written in November 1954, in which the creature is taken back to San Diego.

4 A very rough, and again very early, sketch of the scientist looking at the newly hatched creature. The creature is more like a dinosaur than the humanoid Ymir in the final film.

5-7 Three sketches showing the final metamorphosis of the Ymir.

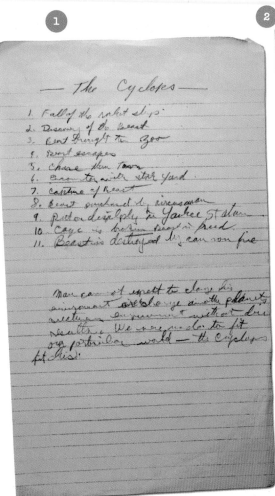

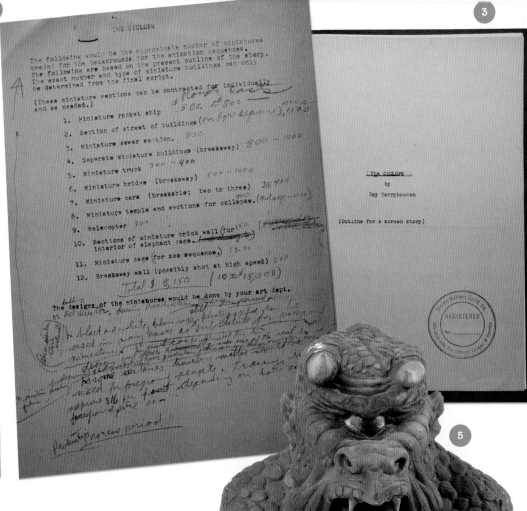

1 A list of key scenes for *The Cyclops*, Ray's first concept for the project. In this initial version the story was set in Chicago and the rocketship came down in Lake Michigan.

2 One of the first step outlines (partially typed and partially hand written) of miniature costs for *The Cyclops*, although on the list is a temple, which would suggest Rome rather than Chicago.

3 The front cover of Ray's outline for *The Cyclops*, which was registered with the Screen Writers Guild.

4 The earliest sketch of the Cyclops, conceived for Ray's initial outline of the story. The creature for this project was changed to an alien being, but Ray was able to use the Cyclops in his next picture, *The 7th Voyage of Sinbad*.

5 A plaster bust of the Cyclops made for this project. Since the first sketch (4) the creature has changed, with the pointed ears replaced by horns, and he now has gills, like the Ymir would have.

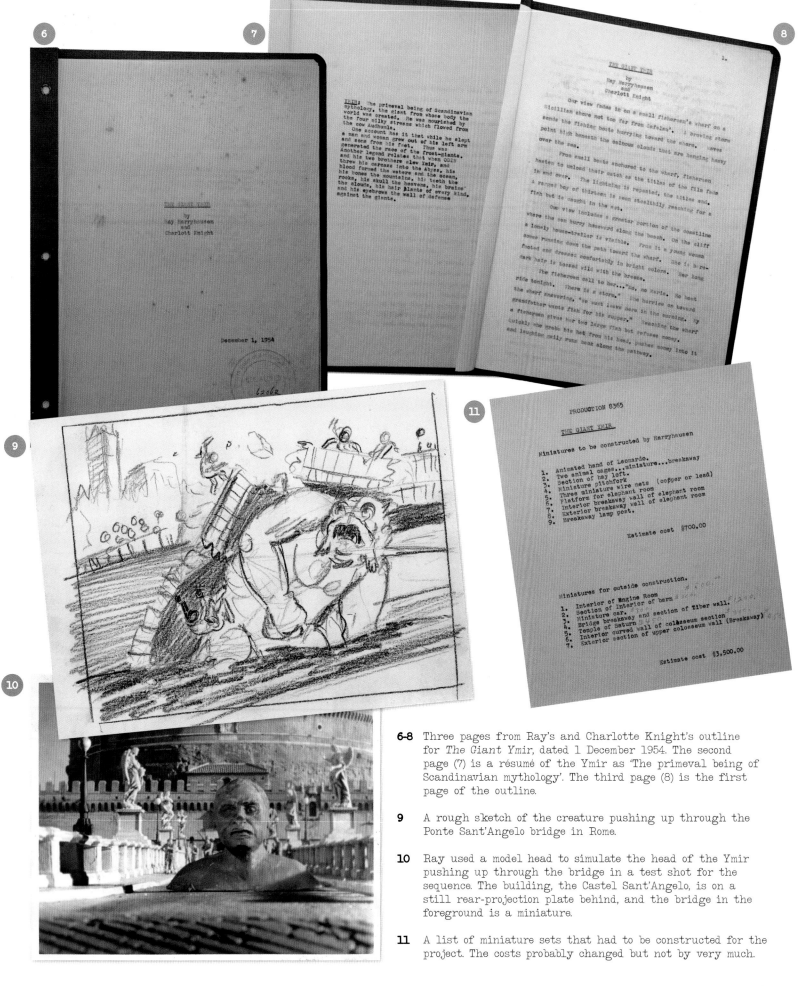

6-8 Three pages from Ray's and Charlotte Knight's outline for *The Giant Ymir*, dated 1 December 1954. The second page (7) is a résumé of the Ymir as 'The primeval being of Scandinavian mythology'. The third page (8) is the first page of the outline.

9 A rough sketch of the creature pushing up through the Ponte Sant'Angelo bridge in Rome.

10 Ray used a model head to simulate the head of the Ymir pushing up through the bridge in a test shot for the sequence. The building, the Castel Sant'Angelo, is on a still rear-projection plate behind, and the bridge in the foreground is a miniature.

11 A list of miniature sets that had to be constructed for the project. The costs probably changed but not by very much.

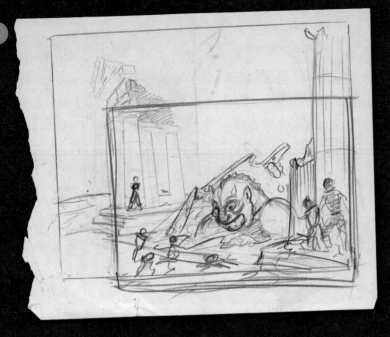

1 Another sketch, this time for an unrealized scene of the creature pushing up through the road outside the zoo, or in actual fact the entrance to the Rome Zoo, in the park of the Villa Borghese.

2 Another unrealized scene. The creature is standing on the Victor Emmanuel Monument in Rome, sometimes called the 'wedding cake'. Ray for a time proposed that the creature might be killed here but changed the location to the Colosseum, which he felt would be a far more spectacular setting.

3 A storyboard of the Ymir's rampage through the Roman Forum and the Colosseum. This board was badly damaged some years ago after a flood in Ray's London home.

4

5

6

4 Full of drama and movement, this is one of a number of key drawings Ray made for the project. It visualizes the fight between the Ymir and an elephant on the streets of Rome.

5 A storyboard of the crashed rocketship and the saving by the local fishermen of the capsule containing the egg of the Ymir. It is interesting to note that we were to have seen another preserved Ymir in this scene, but Ray thought it was more dramatic to leave that revelation until the creature has hatched.

6 The key drawing of the crashed rocketship.

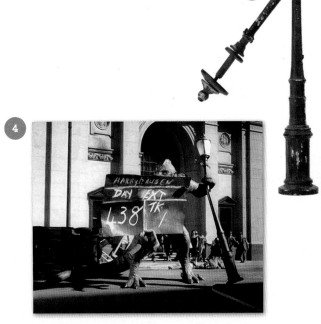

1   Ray with a thirsty Larry Butler, who was head of
    the special effects department at Columbia, during
    location photography in the Colosseum.

2-3 A test shot for a scene in which the Ymir stands
    on top of the Colosseum, with soldiers approaching
    in the foreground. In 2 can be seen the matte line
    on the top edge of the Colosseum, into which the
    Ymir model would be inserted and animated. 3 is the
    combined image.

4   A frame grab from the test reels found in the LA garage.
    This shows the slate (No 438) of the model Ymir running
    amok on the Rome streets.

5   A frame grab from the final scene in the film, with the
    Ymir holding a human and grabbing a lamppost.

6   The original miniature lamppost seen in 4 and 5. Made of
    metal alloy, it could be bent easily.

7-15 Various frames from the recently rediscovered test footage.

7 Ray holding the slate for the scene in which the rocketship is about to crash in the sea.

8-9 The crashed rocketship. Note the rear-projection screen at the top and how the model, which hangs on wires, extends beyond the screen.

10 Just after the birth of Ymir. This is one of Ray's most moving sequences as the young, recently hatched creature, stretches and adjusts to his environment, watched over by the scientist and the young woman.

11-12 Two test shots of the Ymir attacking the farmer in the barn.

13 A test shot of the Ymir behind the miniature Temple of Saturn in the Roman Forum.

14 The fight with the elephant against the entrance to the Villa Borghese park zoo. The matte line for this sequence was vertically down the edge of the gate column on the left and along the street below the feet of the Ymir and elephant.

15 A frame with slate of the creature clinging to the top of the Colosseum, just before it plunges to its death.

Mysterious Island (1961)

This was based on Jules Verne's 1874 novel *Mysterious Island*, the sequel to *20,000 Leagues Under the Sea* (1870). Apart from a balloon flight, the later novel didn't really have the excitement of its predecessor, so Ray made a few modifications. Amongst these were a lost civilization, a man-eating plant, dinosaurs, a working robot, and giant creatures, most of which resulted from experiments by Captain Nemo. Although the final film didn't feature all of the planned additions, it includes some of Ray's most enduring creatures — the giant crab (bought in Harrod's Food Hall), the phororhacos (a prehistoric giant bird), giant bees and a nautiloid cephalapod (a prehistoric shell octopus). In addition Ray designed Nemo's Nautilus submarine and a volcanic explosion which destroys the island.

NEWS from

CHARLES H. SCHNEER'S

"MYSTERIOUS ISLAND"

BASED ON THE
JULES VERNE NOVEL

in **SUPER DYNAMATION**
TECHNICOLOR®

LON JONES
Director of Publicity

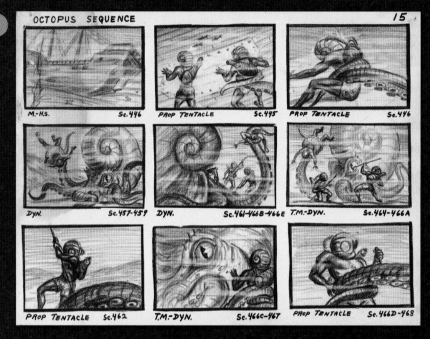

OCTOPUS SEQUENCE   15

M.-H.S. Sc.446	PROP TENTACLE Sc.445	PROP TENTACLE Sc.446
DYN. Sc.457-459	DYN. Sc.461-466B-466E	T.M.-DYN. Sc.464-466A
PROP TENTACLE Sc.462	T.M.-DYN. Sc.466C-467	PROP TENTACLE Sc.466D-468

Notes on Mysterious Island   Dec. 5th 1958

I.   Escape from Richmond in Balloon.

    A.   Balloon Drifts to island.

        1.   Balloon lands on island.

        2.   Harding is discovered.

    B.   Castaways hunt for food.

        1.   Discover giant crab.

        2.   Kill, cook and eat crab.

    C.   Discover the hut in undergroth covered with vines uninhabited for years. Find trunk, diary, history of another castaway. Tree calender. (gradual shading near end of diary where author becomes incoherent he feels he is loosing his mind..resorting back to the animal.

    D.   Continue on treck to mountain.

        1.   Discover crevse....leads to shaded area... valley of mushrooms and fungus. should discover vegatation gradually as plants change size and appearance.

            a.   hear groans...find greenman in clutches of large man eating funguis.

            b.   save green man...try to make friends... communicate etc.

            c.   leave valley...green man follows. Harding feels if they lead him back to the hut he may remember some of his past. this helps a little   All resign themselves for long stay on island.

    E.   Inject discovery of trunk washed into lagoon. contains sextant, guns amunition, bible. etc.

    F.   Should pass by section of steep cliff which later becomes Granit House.

    G.   Group continues their climb to top of mountain. Green man follows them. Stays some distance behind but seems to want to become part of the gregareous group.

        1.   Reach top of crater. Discover they are on island.

        2.   See mountain goats. want one for goat milk, butter etc.

            a.   Herbert has already sprained his ankle...stays behind near top of crater. Rest of group go after goats.

1   The original armatured model of the nautiloid cephalopod that featured in the underwater sequence. The model is in good condition today but when Ray left Shepperton Studios after filming, he left the shell behind as it was too heavy. The shell seen here was made by a restorer to Ray's specifications.

2   Artwork for the publicity handout, which was based on one of Ray's key drawings, and put together by Lon Jones, a great publicist who was also a personal friend of Ray's.

3   One page of Ray's notes for the key story elements of an early outline, dated 5 December 1958.

4   Part of the storyboard for the attack of the nautiloid cephalopod.

5   An early pencil sketch of the nautiloid cephalopod fighting with the divers, on which Ray based the final key drawing for the sequence.

6   The key drawing for the Granite House.

ADW/JV   5.9.60

RAYMOND ANZARUT, Esq.   ADRIAN GORHEN
c.c. Mr. Charles Schneer
    Mr. Ray Harryhausen
    Mr. Wally Veevers
    Mr. A. Malley
    Mr. J. Wilson
    Mr. Bill Rule
    Mr. Eric Andrews

                    "MYSTERIOUS ISLAND"

        In reply to your memos of August 29th to Mr. Rule and myself,
Wally Veevers now has seven painted matte shots.   The estimated total
cost is £900, and the final delivery date for completion of the
seven shots will be in approximately seven weeks' time.

                    Adrian D. Gorker

110

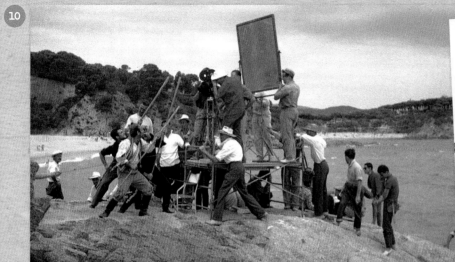

1 In one of the first scripts the adventurers discover an ancient roadway that leads to a partially sunken city made up of various ancient civilizations. This key drawing shows the underwater city, which is seen in the film, but is predominantly Egyptian.

2 Ray's key drawing for the first sight of the island and its smouldering volcano.

3 Actor Percy Herbert relaxing in the Spanish sunshine between takes.

4 Michael Callan also grabs some rest, whilst his next scene is set up.

5 Charles Schneer and Ray in a publicity shot for the film.

6 Michael Craig, who was excellent as Captain Cyrus Harding, the main character in the story.

7 Herbert Lom, who played Captain Nemo. In Ray's view Lom was a perfect Nemo.

8 An internal memo concerning the seven matte paintings for the film by Wally Veveers, which cost a total of £900.

9 At the end of filming Mysterious Island, a relaxed shot of Ray working at home on one of his key drawings for his next project, Jason and the Argonauts.

10 On location in Spain and filming the live-action fight with the giant crab. Ray can be seen to the left of the camera.

11 The full-size claw of the giant crab being set up for a shot. Michael Craig is in the centre foreground with Ray just behind him in a wide-brimmed hat. Charles Schneer is on the right, walking away.

12 The pirates' ship, from the side that the camera would never see. On the stern has been built a raised deck area to make it look like a nineteenth-century sailing ship.

13 Gary Merrill, who played the cynical Gideon Spilitt.

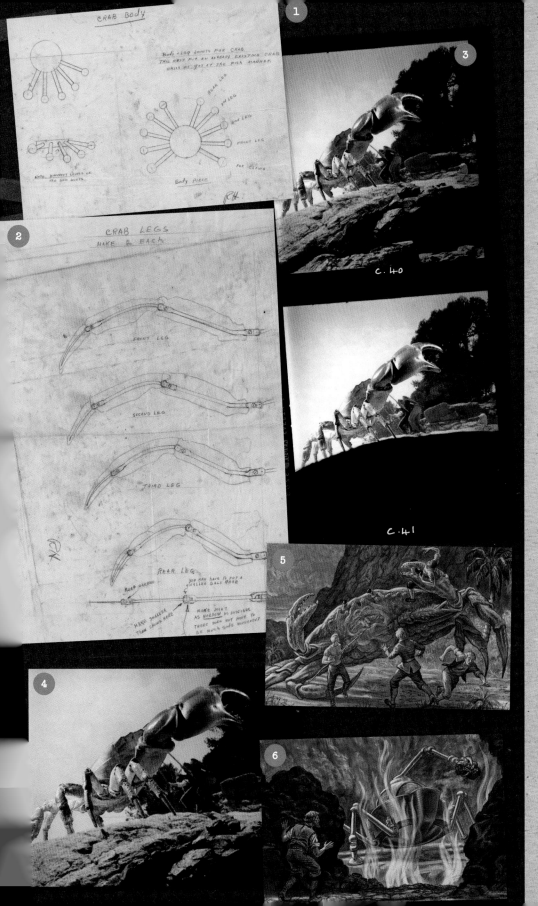

1 Ray's armature design for the main body of the crab, which he sent to his father so he could construct the ball and socket joints. Ray's note on the right says: 'Body and leg joints for crab. This must fit an already existing crab which we got at the fish market.'

2 Ray's designs for the crab legs, also sent to his father, with instructions to make two of each.

3 Two shots of the men trying to flip the crab over. In the lower image we can see the matte line on which Ray placed the crab model.

4 Although a test shot for colour balance, this illustrates the combination of live action (see image 10 on page 111) and animation (see 3 above).

5 One of Ray's greatest drawings. The giant crab attacking four men.

6 A key drawing for a sequence that was never realized in the final film. It shows one of the castaways looking at a robotic digger being controlled by Nemo to extract minerals from the volcano for his work.

7 One page of Ray's notes on the travelling mattes that were required for the film. On this page is detailed the live-action travelling matte filming for shots that would be edited into the balloon sequence.

8 Filming one of the balloon travelling matte scenes against the yellow screen, which would then be combined with a background of sea and sky.

9 Another of Ray's key drawings, this time for the dramatic balloon sequence. As the balloon approaches the island the gas escapes, taking the travellers nearer to a potential watery grave.

10 Two pages of the rough storyboard for the phororhacos sequence, in which the prehistoric bird attacks the survivors and then falls down dead, killed by Nemo's bullet.

11 Another more defined storyboard for the phororhacos sequence. In this the survivors stumble on the creature and try to capture it. This storyboard was badly damaged in a flood.

12 A badly damaged design by Ray for the metal armature for the phororhacos. This, the storyboards and a key drawing are all that remain of this creature.

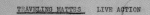

1.

TRAVELING MATTES   LIVE ACTION

BALLOON SEQUENCE

Scene 43   INT. BALLOON BASKET   NIGHT
            Escapees cling desperately to rim of wildly swaying
            basket.
                1. Men in basket shot against sodium light
                2. BG Shoot plate on location with crane.

Scene 46   INT. BALLOON BASKET   NIGHT
            Basket smashes chimney.
                1. Men in basket shot against sodium light.
                2. BG plate shot on break away miniature.

Scene 50-53 CLOSE INTERCUTS MEN IN BALLOON BASKET   NIGHT
            Storm clouds and roaring winds.
                1. Men in basket shot against sodium light.
                2. BG plate storm clouds   pp or X

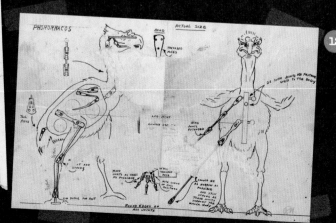

First Men in the Moon (1964)

The posters for this film had to emphasize that it was about the first men *in* the Moon and not *on* the Moon. Especially as plans were being made around that time by NASA to land a man on the Moon.

The story is an enjoyable Victorian adventure, by H.G. Wells, about a man who invents an anti-gravity liquid, and with a companion travels to the Moon only to discover a race of beings living beneath the surface.

Ray had wanted to make it since the late 1930s, but couldn't find a way of resolving the fact that science had advanced to such a degree that we more or less knew what the lunar surface was like even before we first visited it. No NASA or Russian telescope had detected evidence of lunar inhabitants. It was the British writer Nigel Kneale who came up with the idea of topping and tailing the story with a modern-day expedition to the Moon, and relating the Victorian story in-between with its destruction of the Selenite civilization. Ray not only designed and animated the inhabitants of the Moon (called Selenites) and the Mooncalves (their chief source of food) but also designed and executed the moonscapes and the alien world beneath. He was assisted in the latter by special effects technician Les Bowie.

H.G. WELLS' ASTOUNDING ADVENTURE IN
DYNAMATION !

COLUMBIA PICTURES
presents a
CHARLES H.
SCHNEER
production

H.G. WELLS'

FIRST MEN
IN THE MOON

IN PANAVISION and LUNACOLOR !

EDWARD JUDD · MARTHA HYER · LIONEL JEFFRIES · NIGEL KNEALE and JAN READ
RAY HARRYHAUSEN · NATHAN JURAN
Associate Producer RAY HARRYHAUSEN · Directed by NATHAN JURAN · A Columbia Film

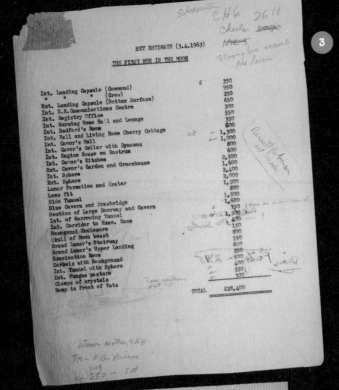

1 Part of a storyboard showing Cavor meeting the Grand Lunar.

2 An early sketch of Cavor and Bedford meeting the Grand Lunar with a beam of light striking the Grand Lunar's throne.

3 A set estimate for the film's interiors and exteriors (full size), all based on Ray's designs. It is hard to believe today that sets, such as the interior of the landing capsule, could actually cost £350, which was just under $600.

4 A letter from Les Bowie's special effects company — Bowie Films Limited — to producer Charles Schneer about their work on the project. Ray had worked with Les on several films, including *Jason and the Argonauts*, and had got on with him well.

1

Motherships 150
Capsule 150
landing strut 50
Moon 250
Sphere sectional 650
Lens Sat. - (inch painting) 100
Lens Complex, pit W.U. 300
Examination Room 400
Solar Motor 500

£ 2450
3
$ 7,350

2

June 29, 1965

FREDERICK W. HARRYHAUSEN

RE: FIRST MEN ON THE MOON - ARMATURES FOR DYNAMATION

1 armature of Mooncalf
8   9 inch armatures of Humanoide ants
6   4½ inch armature of Professorial type ant.
6   4½ inch armatures of Soldier type ants.

Total $5,200

1st payment of $2,600 Due July 15, 1965
2nd payment of $2,600 Due upon completion

Payment to be made to:
Frederick W. Harryhausen

3

Telephone: Telegrams:
GERRARD 207775.   "CENBOFILM, PHONE, LONDON."

BRITISH BOARD OF FILM CENSORS

President: THE RT. HON. LORD MORRISON OF LAMBETH, P.C.   3, SOHO SQUARE,
Secretary: JOHN TREVELYAN, C.B.E.   LONDON, W.1.

PRIVATE AND CONFIDENTIAL

JT/MC   26th September, 1963

Charles H. Schneer Esq.,
Ameran Films Limited,
Suite One,
13 Wigmore Street,
W.1.

Dear Charles,

We have now read your final draft script entitled "FIRST MEN IN THE MOON". The question of category presents a bit of a problem here. We think that on the whole the script would be all right for the "U" category up to about Page 86, but that from this point on there it is almost certain that your film will give us trouble for the "U" category. This means that we may have to give you an "A" certificate. The trouble is of course that your moon-creatures must be rather spooky and unearthly to be effective, and must create some degree of fear in the audience. If there is more fear than young children can take we must put the film into the "A" category.

Our comments on points of detail are as follows:

Pages 87-92. Scenes 207D-233D
Here we have miscellaneous fighting with Selenites. These scenes may give trouble, especially those with the "Soldier Selenites."

Page 97. Scene 256D
There are more Selenites on the space-sphere.

Page 98. Scene 263
Three hideous Selenite heads peer in on Kate, who is alone in the sphere. Scene 264 she fires at them. This scene may be troublesome.

Page 100-103. Scene 277D-306D (C)
The huge caterpillar-like mooncreats rear up and rampage about fighting people and breaking the crystals of the scintillating caverns in which all this takes place. This should be pretty terrifying for young children.

Page 104. Scene 307D
Here we see the head of a new kind of Selenite - the "intellectual" - which is examining Kate. In scene 307D we see her skeleton from its viewpoint as it looks through a giant microscope. More possibility of trouble here.

........./

2.

Page 109. Scenes 323D-324D
Here the moonbeast has been entirely stripped of its flesh, which is being carried off by Selenites. We see its huge skull and later in Scene 328D. This sounds a bit like "X" horror stuff, but I suppose it may be all right.

Pages 116-120, Scenes 355D-373 and elsewhere
There are some ghostly shots and rather alarming shots of the cocooned scientist Selenites who have been wrapped up till needed; In scene 373 there is also a shock shot of Cavour's hand touching Bedford. These are possible points of trouble.

Page 123. Scene 384D and elsewhere
This scene need not be too frightening but we have had creatures of this kind being cut out of "U" films fairly often, and we hope that they will not look nearly as bad as our old friend the Cyclops, which gave both you and me a lot of trouble.

Page 126. Scene 399
The Grand Lunar is shown as a massive, pulsating brain on a tiny body. I have no idea what this will look like but it could be rather frightening for the young.

Page 136. Scene 449.
When we last see Cavour he is being overwhelmed by Selenites. We would not want to see any shots of him being obviously killed, and these scenes will of course depend on the extent to which we have accepted the Selenites in previous scenes.

I am sure you will feel from recent experience that it would be to your advantage commercially to go for the "U" category, but at the same time I think that if you attempt to do this you may weaken your film to such an extent as to make it less attractive for world distribution. So perhaps in this instance you may feel that it would be wiser to aim for the "A" category, which would give you rather more freedom.

I return your script herewith.

Yours sincerely,

John
Secretary.

4

5

1403.

1404

6

1410

529

530

1895

1 Ray's rough estimate for various effects for the project.

2 Dated 29 June 1963, this is the invoice from Ray's father,
   Fred Harryhausen, for manufacturing the armatures for
   various creatures that Ray had designed for the project.

3 Two pages of a letter from the British Board of Film
   Censors, dated 26 September 1963, pointing out that there
   were some scenes in the screenplay that may suggest the
   film might not get the desired U certificate in Britain.

4 Ray remembers that everyone seemed to get on very well
   on the production. Here are the three main actors – Lionel
   Jeffries, Martha Hyer and Edward Judd – having a knees-up
   for the camera.

5 H.G. Wells' son Frank Wells talking with Martha Hyer
   during filming at Shepperton Studios.

6 Another shot of Frank Wells, talking with Ray and Charles
   Schneer. Ray remembers Wells as a gentle and lovely man.

7 An unusual shot of actor Edward Judd in his heavy, old-
   age makeup, watched over by director Nathan 'Jerry' Juran,
   who had previously directed *20 Million Miles to Earth* and
   The 7th Voyage of Sinbad for Ray and Charles. Jerry would
   remain a close friend of Ray's until his death in 2002.

8 Standing in front of the full-size sphere, Ray, Charles and
   Jerry imitate the three wise monkeys – see no evil, speak no
   evil, hear no evil.

9 Jerry on the Shepperton Moon set with an uncomfortable-
   looking Lionel Jeffries, suspended in an aerial harness.

10 The model Mooncalf in its miniature set.

1   The magnificent full-size moonscape set at Shepperton Studios.

2   A test colour shot of a Mooncalf. Ray tried not to animate too many
    of the feet as it would have taken too much time.

3   Four of the professional Selenites animated in front of a rear-
    projection screen of Martha Hyer and Lionel Jefferies. This is a
    70mm test for the picture.

4   The one and only Lionel Jeffries, who Ray considered one of the
    best actors ever to appear in his films. They both spent some time
    talking about remaking Alexander Korda's 1936 film *The Man Who
    Could Work Miracles*.

5-11 Various 70mm test images.

5   The first real glimpse of the moonscape matted in behind the sphere and the emerging Lionel Jeffries.

6   Edward Judd hanging from a ledge over the almost bottomless shaft. Judd was shot against a blue screen and the shaft added later.

7   Edward Judd and Lionel Jeffries stare at the Moon's interior, which includes a Mooncalf in the distance.

8   The worker Selenites kill the Mooncalf after it attacks Cavor.

9-10 Two shots of the Grand Lunar's audience chamber. Image 9 shows a partial matte of the aperture where the Grand Lunar sits, and image 10 is a combined shot of the Grand Lunar behind his shield, with the professional Selenites and Lionel about to climb the steps in order to talk with the Grand Lunar.

11   A photograph taken by Ray of one of the professional Selenites just after the models were made. Although this model still exists it is in very poor condition.

People of the Mist (1983)

This was an unrealized project for which Ray executed many sketches, key drawings and clay models for British producer/director Michael Winner. The screenplay was loosely based on an obscure novel by Victorian author Sir H. Rider Haggard, about a forbidden Land of the Mist in Africa, which is inhabited by a lost tribe as well as prehistoric and alien creatures.

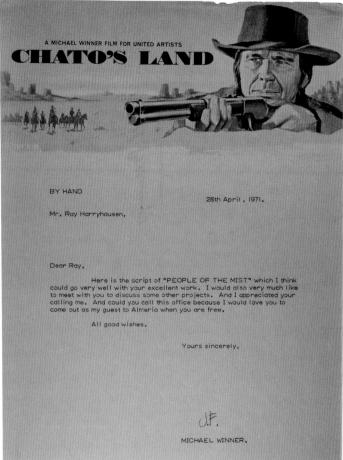

A MICHAEL WINNER FILM FOR UNITED ARTISTS

CHATO'S LAND

BY HAND

28th April, 1971.

Mr. Ray Harryhausen,

Dear Ray,

Here is the script of "PEOPLE OF THE MIST" which I think could go very well with your excellent work. I would also very much like to meet with you to discuss some other projects. And I appreciated your calling me. And could you call this office because I would love you to come out as my guest to Almeria when you are free.

All good wishes.

Yours sincerely,

J.F.

MICHAEL WINNER.

January 4, 1983   Outline

Re-structure PEOPLE OF THE MIST

I.   The auction sale of Otram Hall.
     A.   Titles over - spaced as indicated.
          1.   Interior Vicarage living room.
               a.   Rev. Beach is upset with Leonard and orders
                    him out of his house.
          2.   Interior Otram Hall.
               a.   Leonard and Tom discuss their future.
                    (1) They make a pact to try to regain
                         Otram Hall.
                    (2) Discuss plans to go to Africa to seek
                         their fortune.
                    (3) In spite of his debts their father
                         managed to leave them a ruby (or diamond)
                         worth quite a lot of money.
                         (a) They decide to sell the ruby to
                              pay for their trip to Africa.
                         (b) They also are left a map, or ,
                              find it among their fathers
                              possessions.
                    (4) Tom is established as a bit of a religious
                         fanatic.   Not far out, but individualistic
                         in his views.

II. Leonard and Tom in Africa.
     A.   They are tied to a pole, bound hand and foot.
     B.   They meet Klondyke (or similar character).
     C.   All escape.
          1.   Natives pursue them.
          2.   Tom is speared as they escape.
          3.   In his delerium from the wounds he delivers a prophecy
               that a woman will help them regain Otram Hall.
          4.   Tom recovers.
     D.   All make their way to some old Roman ruins in the jungle.
          (location in Algeria.)
          1.   A strange animal charges from the bush pursuing
               a woman called SOA.   She is almost killed but
               saved by a shot from Leonard's gun.
          2.   Discovery of other rubies (or diamonds) in SOA's hand.
               a.   They discuss the strange animal that pursued SOA.
               b.   Also discuss the source of the rubies.
                    (1) Leonard decides to show SOA the map.
                         She reacts strangely.
               c.   Leonard makes pact with SOA to take him
                    to the source of the rubies in exchange
                    for his help to try to release "her baby-Juanna"
                    from the slavers.
               d.   SOA leads them to the slave camp at the other
                    end of the ruined city.

III. Slavers camp and square.
     A.   Leonard and group observe camp from distance. SOA sees her
          "baby, Juanna" among the slaves.
          1.   They witness an auction of slaves. SOA sees her
          2.   The group plan their strategy for Juanna's release.
     B.   Juanna is sold as a slave.
          1.   Leonard, Tom, Klondyke release slaves.

... egyptian ruins. Perhaps caves in the side of a
hill.
          2.   Leonard and group are most disturbed at finding
               a live dinosaur in the 19th century.

          d.   Spears from every direction plunge into the
               hanging, kicking lizard.   Just as the natives
               shout in triumph they all hear something and
               turn to see something o.s.   They go down on their
               knees and bow reverantly.
          e.   Leonard and group turn to see strange lights
               moving through the bush - they suddenly disappear.

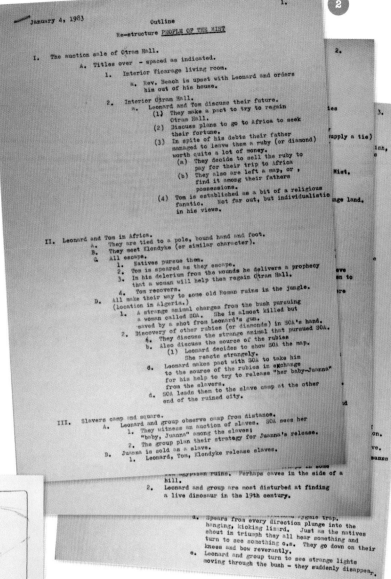

1 We previously thought that this project was started in the early 1980s but this letter, again found in LA, seems to confirm that Winner first made contact with Ray in 1971, probably whilst *The Golden Voyage of Sinbad* was in pre-production.

2 Three pages of Ray's outline for the restructure of *People of the Mist*, dated 4 January 1983, twelve years after Winner first contacted Ray.

3-4 Two sketches of the ancient city square in the story with giant birds waiting to be ridden by their riders.

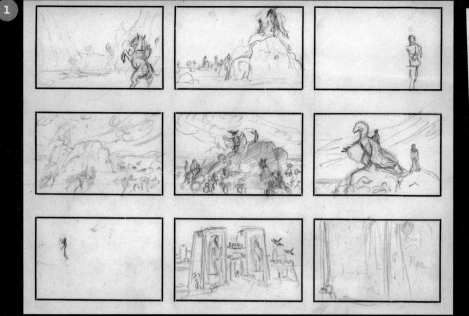

1. A rough storyboard of an encounter with the giant flying birds and their riders.

2. A clay figure of the sacrificial statue from which maidens would be cast off into a lake filled with prehistoric plesiosaurs.

3. A sketch of the entrance into the city of the people of the mist.

4. A page of sketches that include a dinosaur with a carriage on its back, and a series of drawings that show a maiden being cast from the huge statue and falling into the mouth of a plesiosaur.

5. A beautiful pre-drawing of men being attacked by a pteranodon, with a couple of sketches of the creature's head at the top of the page. This was an idea that Ray had had for the 1949–50 unrealized project *Valley of the Mist*.

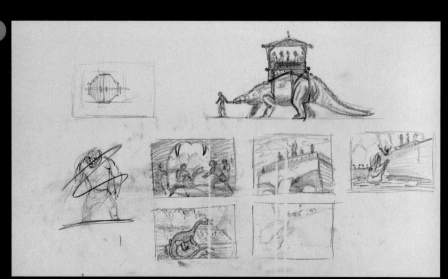

6 Another series of drawings and sketches for the project. They include alien creatures attacking a city wall.

7 The alien creature in more detail. Ray designed it as part-lizard with elements of dinosaurs.

8 A sketch of a huge dinosaur-like creature being attacked by two smaller creatures.

9 Ray often came up with rough ideas for posters to impress the money-people. In this one for *People of the Mist*, almost every element of the story – dinosaurs, flying birds, a volcano and a collapsing statue – is thrown in. Ray always had a strong interest in how his films were promoted.

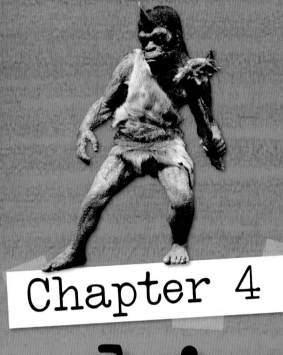

Chapter 4

Arabian Nights

Almost as soon as he learned how to animate, Ray had wanted to bring a skeleton to life. But how could he use this concept for a full-length film? Eventually he hit on the idea of a skeleton fighting Sinbad, the legendary figure from *The Arabian Nights*. From that he developed a rough outline and a number of key drawings for a story he called *Sinbad the Sailor*. This formed the basis for the film *The 7th Voyage of Sinbad*, released in 1958 to huge acclaim. Almost twenty years later he resurrected the character for *The Golden Voyage of Sinbad*. That too was a success and was quickly followed by *Sinbad and the Eye of the Tiger*. There were several unrealized Sinbad projects, including an unnamed adventure in which the hero encounters dinosaurs, a space story called *Sinbad Goes to Mars*, and finally, in the early 1980s, *Sinbad and the 7 Wonders of the World*. Regrettably there are no drawings or models for these lost projects.

The 7th Voyage of Sinbad (1958)

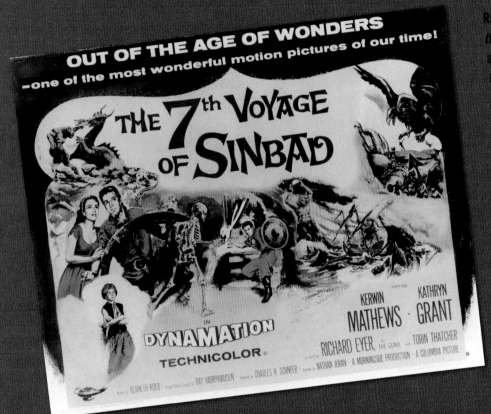

Ray's original step outline for the project he called *Sinbad the Sailor* (1953/54) included many key scenes that appeared in the final film, from the giant Roc bird and the Cyclops to the skeleton fight. He executed several key drawings but all the producers he approached felt that costume adventures were passé. In 1955 Ray went to see *Son of Sinbad*, an RKO colour extravaganza, which left him disappointed because although the Roc and other creatures were referred to by the actors, none were ever shown. Now convinced that his version would be a success, he showed his outline and drawings to producer Charles Schneer, who felt the project had great potential. Columbia sanctioned the production and Kenneth Kolb was appointed to write the screenplay, which he called *The Adventures of Sinbad*. This was changed to *The 7th Voyage of Sinbad* after Ray suggested using the number seven for its mystical connotations.

SINBAD THE SAILOR

Early step outline
by Ray H. for
7th VOYAGE

I. INTRODUCTION
 A. Introduction of Porter carrying wood.
  1. He stops outside Sinbad's house
   and envies Sinbad of his riches.

 B. Introduction of Sinbad
  1. Invites porter into his home to tell him
   the story of the hardships he went through
   to gain his riches.

  2. Flash back to when he was a young man in search of
   the Valley of Diamonds.

II. OUT TO SEA
 A. Tells of being out to sea for days--without food.

 B. We are introduced to members of the crew who
  later become his friends.

 C. Finally spot land.
  1. Search island for food.

III. ROC SEQUENCE
 A. Come across gigantic egg.
 B. They break it open and drag out the baby bird.
  1. They kill it and eat it for food.
  2. They see the Parent birds coming toward them and
   take to their ship.

  3. Shot of them rowing for dear life to the ship.

  4. Birds discover that their young has been killed by
   the sailors.

  5. Crew and Sinbad arrive on board and prepare to sail
   as gigantic birds attack the ship.
   a. Soon they disappear but return with large rocks
    in their claws.
   b. They drop the mmmkm one rock near the ship causing
    a tremendous wave and splash.
   c. The second rock is droped right in the center of
    the ship. It goes right through it breaking the sh
    ship into. (Use air diving views of Roc coming
    toward ship)

  6. Ship sinks

   a. Sinbad and two crew members are the only ones
    saved. They are washed up on shore of a
    strange land.

IV. FIND AN OLD INN
 A. They askf about the Valley of Diamonds and how to locate it.
  1. The propritor fill them with fearfull tales about the
   dangers they will run across

---

  2. Tells them about the Dragon . Tells them that
   the only way to get to the Valley of Diamonds is
   through the Fortress of Fear. Once you pass
   the Fortress of Fear all is easy going.
   But you will have to fight Death to gain the fields
   of diamonds.

 B. This Frightens Sinbads companions so that they flee out
  into the night. But Sinbad is determined to see it through.

  1. The Inn keeper gives Sinbad a room and bed in which to
   sleep. The room is filled with spiders but This does
   not stop Sinbad. He tosses them out the window and
   goes to sleep.

 C. Next morning he starts on his long journey in search of
  The Fortress of Fear.

  1. Meets up with the Dragon. Has tremendous battle
   with it but finally over comes it.

  2. Goes through the cave and finds the Fortress of Fear
   blocking the enterance of the Valley of Diamonds.

V. FORTRESS OF FEAR

 A. Enters the crumbling castle.
  1. The sculpturedastatues look at him as he mounts the stairs.
  2. He opens the door and it crumbles before him.

 B. Sees large Toad and follows his slimy trail up the stairs.
  1. Stairs crumble behind him making it impossible toretreat

 C. He meets up the the Lord of Fear and his family.

  1. He overcomes them. Possibly has to duel with the lord
   himssaf. when he over comes the lord of Fear
   the great castle crumbles to the ground. As the back
   wall falls away we see the Diamonds in the Valley
   behind the castle. He enters and meets a hooded figure

 D. The Hooded figure is Death.

  1. He has an encounter with a skeleton and fights him
   with his sword.

  2. He slays death and the Diamonds are his.

VI. BACK TO SINBADS HOME

  1. He is an old man and is just completing his story

  2. Conclusion

I - Land on back of whale
II Fight with dragon
III Transported by tying himself to foot of bird
IV Find egg
V Roc's dop stones on ship in reprisal
VI Climax — Dueling with death in Valley of
    Diamonds

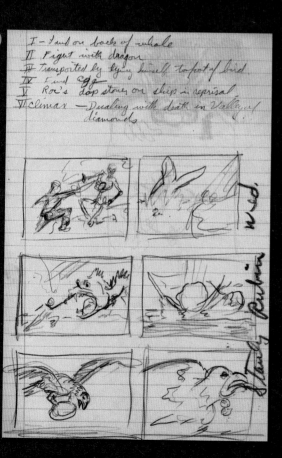

FORM 11-7 100 RMS. 7-56

INTER-OFFICE COLUMBIA COMMUNICATION

To _____ RAY HARRYHAUSEN _____   From _____ Charles H. Schneer

Attention of _____   By _____

In Regard to _____ "Sinbad" - dynamation   Date _____ July 23, 1958

   Dynamation is a new photographic process in
color combining live action backgrounds and/or fore-
grounds with principal actors in combination with
THREE DIMENSIONS figurines insuring a realistic illusion of natural
movement.

   This combination of filming is called
Dynamation.

                                    C.H.S.

---

1 The two undated pages of Ray's earliest step outline for *Sinbad the Sailor*. It includes the baby Roc, two parent Roc birds, a dragon, a fight with a skeleton, a huge toad and a Valley of Diamonds. Only the last two failed to make it into the film.

2 We believe this pre-dates Ray's step outline. It shows six dramatic rough sketches - a skeleton fight, a whale's fluke, a dragon, rocks dropped on Sinbad's boat by a Roc, a Roc with a boulder and the baby Roc hatching. Above those are five key scenes leading up to the climax of 'dueling with death' - the skeleton fight.

3 Dated 23 July 1958, this is a memo from producer Charles Schneer advising Ray of his suggested name for Ray's idea of integrating models with live action - 'Dynamation'.

Animation Effects Budget
Sinbad the Sailor

PRe-production, Supervision, animation
  of effects, continuity drawings etc.

Includes
  Flexable figure armatures and machine
  work.(Animated models)
  Utilities & Rent, etc. $ 40,000.00

Flexable costs based on 30 week shooting period.

Ass. Cameraman	180.95 per wk.		5,428.50
Prop Foreman	212.18 per wk.		6,365.40
Extra help	212.18 per wk		6,365.40
Payroll taxes	3 men	approx.	600.00
Material			2,500.00
Travel to foreign location (2 trips)			4,500.00
Miniatures sets.			10,000.00
			$ 35,759.30
			40,000.00
			$ 75,759.30

Sinbad the Sailor

1. Sea monster attacks ship.

2. Swims to island of Giants
   (one eyed giants)

"Basis for Sinbad continuity"

Cyclops raids local town
taking the Kings daughter back to
his island. Sinbad and hords
of horsemen pursue — Trap cyclops
but he gets away to his boat.

Sinbad must find the island of
cyclops to try to retrieve Kings
daughter.

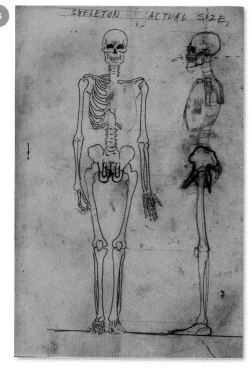

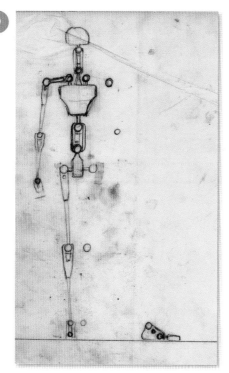

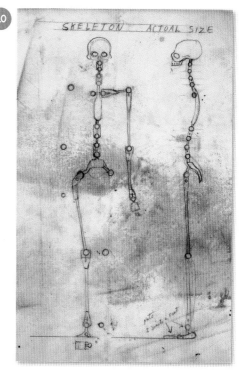

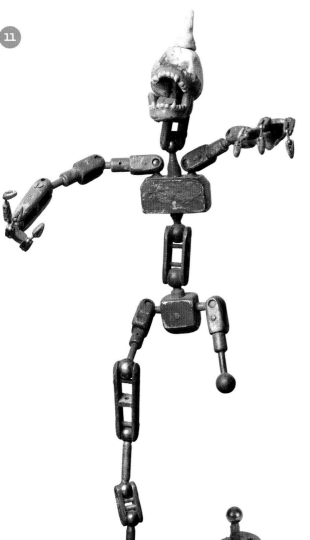

1 Ray's first sketch for the proposed Valley of Diamonds, which was in his first step outline. The sequence was dropped from the final screenplay.

2 An undated but very early budget for animation and effects for *Sinbad the Sailor*.

3 Another rough sketch, showing an unrealized idea for Sinbad's ship sinking after the giant Roc has dropped a boulder onto it. In the margin is perhaps the first rough sketch for the skeleton armature.

4 A very early sketch for the head of the dragon.

5 Two sketches of two gigantic ruined stone Cyclops' heads that the sailors would discover when they land on the island of Colossus. Sadly this idea was again dropped.

6-7 These two cards contain Ray's earliest ideas for the project and include the first reference to the Cyclops and the creature raiding the mainland and kidnapping the Princess. Another idea that wasn't used.

8-10 Three sections of Ray's designs for the skeleton, showing the detail he required in the armature to allow for flexibility.

11 All that is left of the Cyclops. This armature was cannibalized by Ray for a subsequent creation. Until recently we assumed that this was all that was left of the model but in the LA garage we found its missing foot (shown below).

12 A 7-inch high model of Sinbad used for when the Cyclops picks up Sinbad from his treasure cave by his heel and for the Roc sequence. This was also rediscovered in the LA garage.

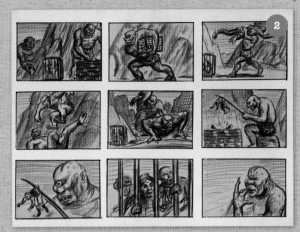

ROC SEQUENCE CONT. 12

CAVE SEQUENCE 17

CAVE SEQUENCE CONT. 18

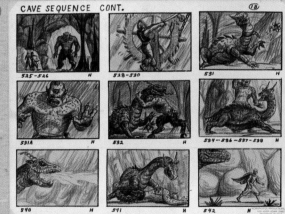

MORNINGSIDE PRODUCTIONS, INC.
1498 NORTH GOWER STREET
HOLLYWOOD 28, CALIFORNIA
HOLLYWOOD 2-3111

PAGE 7
SCENE 37

SCENE 376 B

1. BACKGROUND TO BE SHOT IN MADRID.

2. T.M. TO BE SHOT IN LONDON.

BLUE BACKING

BLUE BACKING

GIRL

BLUE BACKING FOREGROUND MATTE

EXTERIOR BEACH 19

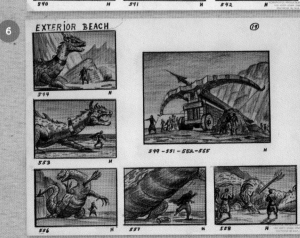

1. The storyboard of the first encounter on the beach with Sokurah the magician, the genie and the Cyclops.

2. The first five illustrations on this storyboard, detailing a fight between two Cyclops, were regrettably unrealized but the final four show Ray's first ideas of how the Cyclops was to roast the sailor. It ends with a close-up of the Cyclops licking its fingers, which doesn't appear in the final film.

3. Part of the storyboard for the Roc sequence, which follows the eating of the baby Roc.

4. Another unrealized sequence, showing giant rats released by Sokurah and chasing Sinbad and Princess Parisa over a rock bridge.

5. A section of the storyboard depicting the fight between the dragon and the Cyclops.

6. The conclusion of the dragon sequence, showing the crossbow killing the dragon and consequently Sokurah.

7. One of a set of travelling mattes designed by Ray in advance of live photography, which were mainly filmed in the UK. This one shows how Princess Parisa will be made to look tiny just before she slips into the mouth of the magic lamp.

8-10 Integrating the miniature crossbow with the actors. Image 8 is a test frame showing an actor standing in front of a full-size wheel on the Spanish beach. This wheel will match that on the 24-inch miniature crossbow. Everything around the top of the wheel and along the beach has been matted out. In image 9 the miniature crossbow is set in place so that it matches with the full-size wheel. Image 10 shows the combined actor, full-size wheel and miniature crossbow.

11-12 Two test frames for the integration of the cave face. Image 11 shows the actors on the beach in Spain facing the lower section of the cave entrance with the above area matted out. Image 12 shows the actors, lower section, and above, the miniature cave face that has now been matted in.

13 Two early rough sketches of the cave and the emerging Cyclops, a scene which takes place near the beginning of the film.

14 A tracing of Ray's first drawing of Sinbad slaying the dragon, on which the final key drawing was based. This tracing paper rendition was found in the LA garage but the original key drawing was lost when Ray left it behind at the studio.

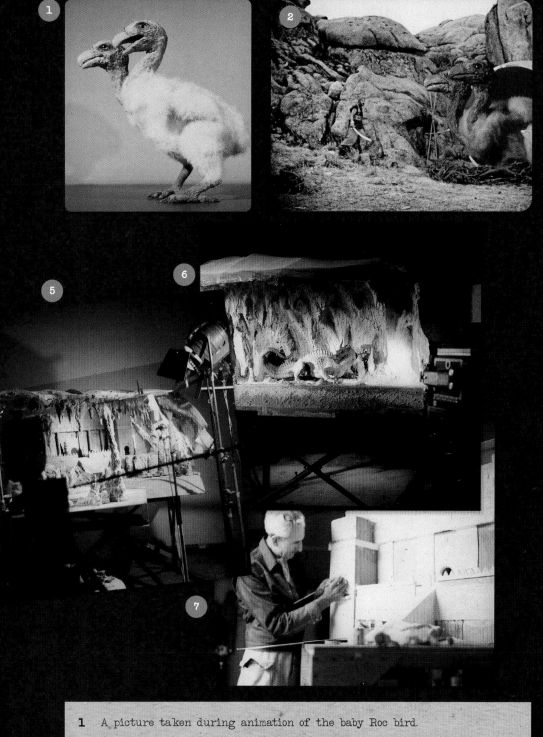

1 A picture taken during animation of the baby Roc bird.

2 The baby Roc in a colour test as it appears in the film after hatching.

3-4 Image 3 shows four frames of 35mm test film, with Ray's handwriting on them. They have turned magenta. Image 4 is one of the frames as colour corrected by Randy Cook. It shows that this is part of the live-action footage of Sinbad and his sailors approaching the cave. The top of the cave face would be added in the studio (see image 12, page 131).

5 The miniature set for the exterior of Sokurah's underground palace.

6 The dragon tied to the retractable chain in the miniature cavern set.

7 A rare picture of George Lofgren during the building of Sokurah's palace, just one of the many miniatures he helped to construct.

8 An early pre-key drawing sketch for the Cyclops roasting the sailor. The Cyclops is different to what would appear on the screen. The key drawing for this scene was also left behind at the studio.

9 A sketch showing a Cyclops mining the Valley of Diamonds; this idea was dropped early on.

10 The dragon and the Cyclops models fight in the confines of the miniature cave set. The underside of the animation table can be seen below.

11 The Cyclops on the animation table holding the tiny Sinbad model (see image 12, page 129) by its leg. Note the fixing for the right foot of the Cyclops under the animation table.

12 The Cyclops looks down at the model sailor on the spit. The camera would have been mounted on the left of the picture so that the miniature spit would have matched the full-sized one on the live-action rear-projection plate behind.

1 A frame from footage found in the LA garage. This shows the slate for the miniature of Sokurah's underground palace and is dated 10 March 1958.

2 A frame from the live-action filming of the full-size palace of Sokurah, which took place in Madrid. It shows the clapperboy holding the clapperboard.

3 Another frame from colour test footage rediscovered in the LA garage, which shows the Cyclops on the beach.

4 A production shot showing Ray, in the foreground and wearing a white hat, overseeing the storm sequence. In front of Ray is a wind machine and on the left is one of the dump tanks that released a flood of water (taken from the harbour) onto the deck of the ship and the actors.

5 The first page of Bernard Herrmann's original score for the Roc fight sequence for *The 7th Voyage of Sinbad*. Ray has written on the top right of the page and bottom left but the remainder is in Herrmann's own hand. This was given to Ray by Bernie soon after the completion of the film.

6 The opening on 23 December 1958 of *The 7th Voyage of Sinbad* at the Roxy Theater in New York. It was what we would now call a real blockbuster.

The Golden Voyage of Sinbad (1973)

SINBAD BATTLES THE CREATURES OF LEGEND
in the miracle of Dynarama

COLUMBIA PICTURES Presents
A CHARLES H. SCHNEER Production

The Golden Voyage of Sinbad

A new dimension in motion picture entertainment
FILMED IN Dynarama

starring
JOHN PHILLIP LAW
CAROLINE MUNRO · TOM BAKER · Screenplay by BRIAN CLEMENS
Music by MIKLOS ROZSA · Creator of Special Visual Effects RAY HARRYHAUSEN
Produced by CHARLES H. SCHNEER and RAY HARRYHAUSEN · Directed by GORDON HE[...]
COLUMBIA PICTURES/A DIVISION OF COLUMBIA PICTURES INDUSTRIES, INC.

GENERAL AUDIENCES
ALL AGES ADMITTED

The genesis of this project dates back to 1963, when Ray executed a number of drawings that he hoped would inspire a new Sinbad story. They included an oracle, a centaur, a dancing Shiva and an homunculus. After *The Valley of Gwangi* was released in 1969 Ray and Charles Schneer looked for another project and decided that a return to Sinbad would be ideal. Ray wrote a rough step outline incorporating elements from his earlier drawings as well as the lost land of Lemuria, a Valley of Vipers, a Fountain of Youth, a six-armed bronze statue, a Cyclopean Centaur and a prince who was transformed into a monkey. This is dated March 1971 and was called *Sinbad's 8th Voyage*. Aside from the Valley of Vipers and the prince/monkey, all the other key sequences were incorporated into the final plotline that became *The Golden Voyage of Sinbad*.

1

1 One of the three Golden masks made by Colin Arthur and worn by the actor Douglas Wilmer, who played the Vizier. Colin cleaned the three masks daily with fine wire wool impregnated with bronze powder to produce a shining golden mask.

2 The first page, dated 3 March 1971, of Ray's original outline for *Sinbad's 8th Voyage*. It contained the first ideas of what would become *The Golden Voyage of Sinbad*.

3 Two pages, dated 7 May 1971, detailing Ray's excellent idea for the opening of *Sinbad's 8th Voyage*. Regrettably this sequence was dropped.

4 An early rough comparison sketch for the Griffin and the Centaur.

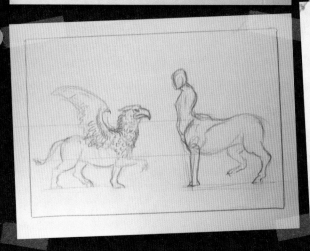

5 Originally Ray had planned to have a dragon threaten Margiana when she is lowered into the pit. However, after making this rough sketch he felt that it would have simply been a repeat of the dragon featured in *The 7th Voyage of Sinbad* so he changed it to the Centaur.

16th November 1971

JOHN VAN EYSSEN   FILE NOTE

SINBAD'S GOLDEN VOYAGE
Screenplay by Brian Clemens
Submitted by Charles Schneer

Must leave certain amount of opposition

The following points detail and expand our general reservations about this screenplay.

1. The opening section before Sinbad's voyage (i.e. 30 pages, about ¼ of the screenplay) is much too long, including as it does a dream sequence, a storm sequence, the pursuit and destruction of the homunculus and the scenes introducing Haroun and Margiana, as well as all the other business out of which the story develops. These basic situations, characters and motivations must be established with much greater economy and impact.

2. Similarly, the ending seems to be stretched out through a series of mini-climaxes from the moment Sinbad and Koura grab the key simultaneously, through their brief fight, the appearance of the Keeper, the battle of the Griffin and Centaur, the killing of the Griffin, the killing of the Centaur, the healing of the Vizier and Margiana, the final death of Koura and at last the conclusion in Marabia.

    At the same time the death of Koura is over-complicated, even confusing, and we miss the simpler more satisfying triumph of a fight to the finish between Sinbad and Koura.   *Trite*

    Don't agree — will be clear when Visual

3. The character of Sinbad is pallid and needs to be more fully motivated and developed. He also needs a more out-going, devil-may-care personality, and generally a larger sense of fun, adventure and humour should pervade the story.   *Don't agree*

4. Some of the scenes appear in rather bad taste, for instance the burning to death of the first homunculus which could easily upset children, and the bartering of Margiana to Sinbad. Moreover, the relationship between Margiana and Sinbad should be more straightforward without the sexual innuendoes.   *Right*

..... / continued

SINBAD'S GOLDEN VOYAGE

MINIATURE SIZE

FOUNTAIN OF DESTINY   (In reality monoliths are about 15' high. 2½ times height of 6' man)

Miniatures:

Height of monolith   80 Cm   (31½")
Width   280 Cm (110")
Depth   214 Cm   (84")
   (Note: Fountain is not round but elliptical)

Height of center water fountain: 130 Cm   (51")
6' man would be   32 Cm (12½") high.

Monoliths set atop of stone elliptical pool approx 40Cm deep (15½"). 20 Cm outer stone rim for step up.   Top of stone elliptical pool is approx 3' wide (91½ Cm).

Approx.   112 –115 CM (44") stone floor in front of elliptical pool.

Circular rock background of cave approximately 15' from outside of top rim of pool.

Miniature set to be built on wooden platform 80Cm (31½") from ground. Special pumps for varrying water height of fountain.

Use   18 to 25 mm lense at 1:85 screen proportion. (also cover height for normal aperture.   This applies to all miniatures)

_____

TEMPLE OF ORACLE   EXTERIOR:
Height from bottom of doorway to top of giant heads and structure is 100 CM (39")   Built to fall in high speed (96 frames per sec.) Explosion at doorway in proportion to set.   Miniature trees to match with painted b.g. and sky.   Part of f.g. green foliage on TM f.g.

3

2.

TEMPLE OF GREEN MEN

Height from base of statue (horizontal line) to top of cliff. 80 Cm (31½") Shoot high-speed because of fire.   Stairs and left f.g. rock group to be on TM f.g.

ROCK BACKGROUND FOR DROP OF CAGE:

Approx 6' high.

SIREN   WHEN STANDING   (full size)
Approx. 235 Cm high (92½")

CARO   WHEN STANDING   (full size)
Approx   228½ Cm (90")

CENTAUR   (full size)
To top of head   9'4" high.
To top of horses hips   5½' high.

GRIFFIN
When sitting   Approx   6'6" high.
Standing   "   8' high.
length   8' long.

Diameter of DAIS OF ORACLE
8' diameter
2' wide rim
20" high off ground.

4

MORNINGSIDE PRODUCTION INC.   SINBAD'S GOLDEN VOYAGE

SHOOTING SCHEDULE - DYNAMATION

W/E	Scene Nos.	Foreground	Background
1972			
Aug 18	Line-up and check backgrounds		
25			
Sept. 1	2, 6, 10 pt	HOMUNCULUS (Flying)	Ext. Sky - Majorca
8	10 comp. 13, 15		
15	20, 21, 65pt.		
22	65 comp. 102, 103.		(Ext. KOURA'S Castle
29	268, 278, 301		(Ext. KOURA'S ship
			(Ext. Bay of Lemuria
			(Ext. Temple of ORACLE
Oct. 6	376, 378	"	Int. Temple of ORACLE
13	380, 382		
20	109, 111, 117, 119, 122, 124	HOMUNCULUS	Int. Lower Chamber
27	261, 262, 265, 267, 328	"	(Int. KOURA'S Cabin
			(Int. Temple of ORACLE
Nov 3	30, 31, 32, 33, 34, 35	HOMUNCULUS (Dream)	Black Velvet (?)
10	538, 539, 544, 546	CENTAUR - MARGIANA	Int. The Pit
17	612, 613, 619, 621, 623	CENTAUR	Int. Cave of Destiny
24	625, 626, 630, 633, 655	"	"
Dec. 1	658, 659, 661, 662, 664	CENTAUR - SALIM	" " "
8	667, 668, 670, 673, 674	CENTAUR - SINBAD	" " "
15	677, 679, 682, 684, 685	CENTAUR - SINBAD	" " "
22	631, 634, 635	CENTAUR - GRIFFIN	" " "
29	636, 638pt.	"	" " "
1973			
Jan 5	638 comp. 641, 642	"	" " "
12	644, 646, 648 part	"	" " "
19	648 comp. 651, 653	"	" " "
26	413, 417, 420, 421, 424, 426	CARO	Int. Green Temple
Feb 2	444, 446, 447, 450, 452	"	" " "
9	454, 457, 458 pt.	"	" " "
16	458 comp. 459, 461	"	" " "
23	463, 465, 467 pt.	"	" " "
Mar 2	467 comp. 468, 469	"	" " "
9	471, 473, 474 pt.	"	" " "
16	474 comp. 475, 477	"	" " "
23	479, 482, 485 pt.	"	" " "
30	485 comp. 486, 489	"	" " "
Apr. 6	197, 199, 201, 203, 206, 208	SIREN - ABDUL	Ext. Deck SINBAD'S Ship.
13	210, 214, 216, 218, 221, 224	SIREN - SEAMAN	"
20	226, 227, 230, 232, 233	SIREN	"
27	314, 316, 318, 320, 321, 333, 324, 325, 327, 330	FIELD OF FORCE	Int. Temple of ORACLE

1 Dated 16 November 1971, this is a
   memo from John Van Eyssen, Columbia
   Pictures' UK Managing Director. Van
   Eyssen makes a number of observations
   that Ray has vigorously challenged in
   the margins.

2-3 Two pages of notes by Ray on the
   required dimensions of the miniature
   sets, which he compiled to enable full-
   size replicas to be made.

4 Now called *Sinbad's Golden Voyage*, this
   is one page of the shooting schedule
   for the Dynamation sequences.

5 The original armatured Figurehead
   model, which has now been restored.
   She is holding the map to Lemuria and
   in front of her is the metal miniature
   boat hook featured in the film.

6 The first rough sketch of the
   Figurehead, showing her wooden
   flaring head of hair, which was based
   on Elsa Lanchester's hair in the 1935
   film *The Bride of Frankenstein*.

7 Ray's key drawing for the dramatic
   fight between the Griffin and the
   Cyclopean Centaur in front of the
   Fountain of Destiny.

1 The original key drawing for the dance of the bronze statue Kali.

2 Ray originally envisioned in this key drawing for the Temple of the Oracle that it would be a step pyramid in the jungle with a huge flight of steps to the summit. In the final film it was much smaller although the four Indian-styled faces were retained.

THE SIREN FIGUREHEAD

3 Ray's original key drawing for Sinbad's approach to the island of
Lemuria. There was a heavy Indian influence as Ray and Charles
Schneer had planned to film the production in India.

4 Ray's key drawing for the Temple of the Green Men, which again has
an Indian influence, as does most of the Lemuria architecture that
is seen in the film.

5 A key drawing showing how the Siren Figurehead will appear on
Sinbad's ship. Ray had conceived the idea of a figurehead coming to
life, even though a Muslim ship would never have featured one.

C-612

6 3 4 - C

1-2 Two views of Sinbad's ship. Made of wood and plaster it was some distance from the sea as it had been built at Studio Verona, Tres Cantos, near Madrid. In image 1 the camera is on a crane and is shooting action on the ship. The Figurehead can just be seen back from the prow. In image 2 the camera is on the extreme right of the picture and the Figurehead can again just be made out behind the right-hand light. The sea can be seen in the distance.

3 John Phillip Law, who played Sinbad, and Charles Schneer, both waiting patiently.

4 Charles Schneer looks on whilst Gordon Hessler, the director, listens to Ray explaining what is required in a particular shot. Ray was impressed with Gordon as he was a director who totally understood Ray's input.

5 John Phillip Law relaxing on the beach whilst the crew set up the next shot. Charles and Ray are at the top of the beach towards the right. Charles is pointing in one direction and Ray is looking in the other.

6 A page from Ray's animation logbook. On it are the technical details for the rear projector, the camera and lighting. Scenes for the Kali sequence – 457, 457A, 452, 22, 447C and 465 – were all shot between 9 and 12 March 1973. Ray's archive contains a number of these logs for films shot between 1966 and 1981.

2 8 7 -

Scene 457. 9-3-73.   Scene 457A : 11-3-73.

Scene 452. 9-3-73.   CS 221.   11-3-73.

Scene 447C. Sinbads Golden Voyage. 9-3-73.

Scene 465 - 12-3-73.

LIGHTING   TYPE.   POS.   F.C.
    2   PUPS   500 WATT   CAMERA LEFT.   1 & GREEN
    2   "   "   "   "   RIGHT.   1 GREEN
    1   INKIE 100   "

PROJECTOR.   RHEOSTAT. Nº 2.
                     FILTER   20 - CJAM.
                     DISTANCE. 18 Ft   FROM SCREEN.
                     LENS   9" INCH.
                     LAMP   750 WATT.

CAMERA.   STOP. F.2.
                     DISTANCE   9 Ft   FROM SCREEN.
                     LENS 100 M.M.
                     FILTER.

SPOTMETER.
PICTURE SIZE.   23" INCHES X 17" INCHES
RATE   MEDIUM CLOSE SHOT.
ACTION. Scene 447C KALI WITH SWORD IN HER HAND.
Scene 465   KALI FORCES SINBAD TO SMALL STAIR CASE.
Scene 452   KALI PREPAIRS HER SWORDS FOR ATTACK.
Scene 457   KALI BATTLES WITH SINBAD AND ALDO.
Scene 457A KALI POISES TO ATTACK SINBAD.
Scene 221   TITLE BACKGROUND. TRAY.

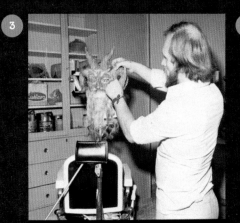

2064

2067

1 Test shot number 420A for the Kali dance sequence, dated 26 January 1973. Note the foreground matte areas for the spilt screen.

2 One of the most tender moments in any of Ray's films is the birth, or the creation, of the homunculus, the eyes and ears of Koura.

3 Special effects makeup artist Colin Arthur works on the plaster positive Oracle mask on a stand in the makeup chair. The mask will be worn by Robert Shaw.

4 Colin with the transparent version of the Vizier's mask, with actor Douglas Wilmer looking concerned. This transparent version was one of several elements involved in producing the final change from the golden mask to the face of the Vizier after the crown is placed on his head.

8

ROUTINE FOR SWORD FIGHT

"SINBAD'S GOLDEN VOYAGE"

I.   FIRST MASTER SHOT: (Center angle)

A.   Kali's dance down stairs. (Cover with close plates)
(Close reactions shots of Koura/greenmen, etc.)

B.   Start of sword fight.

   1. Sinbad moves towards Koura on stairs but is stopped by Kali -
      Kali advances - Sinbad retreats. End with Sinbad being pushed away.
   2. Cassim charges into picture - few blows - is killed.
      (Cover iwth close shots of Rachid and Omar as they see what has
      happened...rush out of picture).
   3. As Cassim is dragged out of picture by Rachid and Omar - Sinbad
      attacks again - leaps onto rock - few blows - jumps up to avoid
      Kali's sword - then jumps to ground - few blow again - is finally
      driven o.s.
      (Cover with close up's and plates).

II.   SECOND MASTER ANGLE: (Side shot near pillar.)
A.   (Close shot Sinbad as he moves towards Cassim's sword on ground near
     Kali o.s.)

B.   Sinbad continues his roll across screen in front of Kali picking
     up the second sword inpassing. He manages to struggle to his feet.

C.   During roll, Rachid enters left - Sinbad starts to fight Kali again
     from right of screen - Rachid stars fight on left.

   1. Rachid finally pushed to pillar left.
   2. Kali turns to Sinabd on right. - brief blows - Sinbad has his
      two swords knocked from his hands - he steps back out of the picture
      to get sword.
      (Close shots and plates to cover).

III. THIRD MASTER ANGLE: (Center long shot)

A.   Omar and Haroun fight each side of Kali.
   1. Omar is wounded - Haroun loses his sword and retreats.

B.   Kali turns to Sinbad who ducks - swings - moves round close to Rachid ...
     Kali facing left. - few more blows.
     (Close ups of Sinbad - Haroun running for brazier - Rachid - plate for Kali.)

9

5   Gordon Hessler and Ray discuss a scene.

6   The great composer Miklós Rózsa conducts his score for the film, which was recorded in Rome. In the centre is Ray, next to the editor Roy Watts, with Rózsa holding the baton and Charles Schneer looking worried on his right.

7   Stunt choreographer Fernando Poggi, who had worked with Ray since before *Jason and the Argonauts*, is on the left wearing glasses and rehearsing for the Kali fight sequence with two other stuntmen.

8   Poggi (left) rehearses John Phillip Law on set for a section of the fight with Kali.

9   Poggi (centre) rehearsing with Martin Shaw on the left and John Phillip Law for a section of the Kali fight. Tom Baker stands aloof at the top of the steps.

10 Part of the fight routine notes for the sword fight with Kali.

Sinbad and the Eye of the Tiger (1977)

The transformation of a prince into a monkey was one of the ideas that had been rejected for *The Golden Voyage of Sinbad*. However, it was to form the basic premise of a project that began life as *Sinbad in Hyperborea – An Adventure Fantasy*, another step outline written by Ray, dated May 1974. Many of Ray's ideas from that outline found their way into the final screenplay by Beverley Cross. They included a baboon prince, an iron man, an evil sorceress called Zenobia, a giant walrus, a sabre-toothed tiger, a Neaderthal man and a mystical pyramid. Although Neaderthal man was to change to Troglodyte, or Trog as he is called in the film, and Neaderthal man's fight with an arsinotherium (a prehistoric rhinoceros-like creature) was also dropped, most of the central sequences are Ray's ideas. As with many of Ray's rough outlines the love interest and conclusion were left to the screenwriters. The key action sequences with his creatures were uppermost in his mind. After two more title changes – *Sinbad Beyond the North Wind* and *Sinbad at the World's End* – the film was finally made as *Sinbad and the Eye of the Tiger*.

June 1974

SINBAD
Beyond the North Wind

An Adventure Fantasy by

RAY HARRYHAUSEN

Treatment by

BEVERLEY CROSS

The Property of:

Ameran Films,
LONDON

2

Random Thoughts

The enclosed outline acts as a possible guide for what
I think will make an exciting adventure fantasy film of
the calibre of THE GOLDEN VOYAGE.

In the interest of time, the human drama has only lightly
been suggested.   Love interest, if necessary, has still
to be developed.

To differ from the other two Sinbad films, I found it
necessary to distribute the heroic acts among several
different characters so as not to fall into the pattern
of the cliché.

The baboon character would be animated in most instances.
To cut the time factor, some long shots could be done with
a child in an ape suit.   The same applies to the metal
man.   Where possible, particularly when rowing, we
would use a very tall man in a robot outfit.   Other shots
of the man of metal would have to be animated.

Neanderthal man would almost certainly have to be fully
animated as well as his brothers.

I think the character of Zenobia could be developed into
an exciting part for someone of the calibre of a Coral
Brown or Viveca Lindsford.   Deliver us from the typical
"blond floosie" who is usually cast in this type of role.
The part of Marzavan would be a natural for Larry Naismith.

Sinbad would have to be moulded into a stronger part than
indicated and balanced out among the other players.
The girl, of course, has just been suggested and has
not been made an intrinsic part of the story.

There are quite a number of high speed miniatures, too
many for my liking.   But I think they are necessary for
variety.   Also it cuts down on the necessary animated
footage.

As you will see, upon first reading, the basic attraction
of the complete project is in the possibilities for exciting
visual development.   The chances for real innate humour
is far greater than in our other Sinbad projects.   This
element could round out the full development of the drama
for a more universal appeal.

Ray Harryhausen

3

SINBAD MEETS THE SABER-TOOTH TIGER

Sc. 687. CLOSE SHOT (DYN) SABER TOOTH
As the smoke melts into the raging animal.
ZENOBIA is now metamorphised into the TIGER

Sc. 688. ANOTHER ANGLE (DYN) THE BEAST
moves off of its pedestal and pads down the
staircase.

Sc. 689. CLOSE MOVING SHOT SINBAD & GROUP
They back away across the floor. SINBAD leaps
forward with his sword to protect FARAH .

Sc. 690. FULL SHOT (DYN) As the great
beast moves toward them.   They slowly back
in the direction of the entrance of the Shrine.

Sc. 691. ENTRANCE (DYN)
TROG lumbers through the opening of the passage
with the iron harpoon in his huge fist.

Sc. 692. ANOTHER ANGLE
(Dyn) The tiger is startled by the entrance
of TROG.

Sc. 693, 696. CLOSE SHOT TIGER (DYN)
As he faces his new adversary . He roars.

Sc. 694. CLOSE SHOT TROG (DYN)
He reacts to the TIGER O.S.

Sc. 695. ANOTHER ANGLE (Similar to
TROG moves forward slamming his great iron
Harpoon down on the floor in front of the TIGER.

137A

1 The cover page of Beverley Cross' treatment for *Sinbad Beyond the North Wind*, which is dated June 1974. The credit 'An Adventure Fantasy by Ray Harryhausen' is an acknowledgement of Ray's original development of the storyline.

2 The undated cover page of Ray's random thoughts on the project. In it he suggests some of the long shots might use a child in a baboon suit and that Neatherthal man (later Troglodyte) would have brothers.

3 A page of the storyboard for the fight between the tiger and Trog, which takes place inside the pyramid.

Funeral Mask of Agamemnon

SINBAD BEYOND THE NORTH WIND

A 1. The Princess - followed by menacing hooded figure - manages to hide aboard Sinbad's ship. Thrown overboard, she is rescued by Sinbad. He agrees to help her.

2. They sail to meet the Sultan and take aboard the cage.

3. Zenobia comes aboard. Threats. The Sultan decides to stay behind to watch her. Sinbad sails to find and consult the Greek.

D 4. In her castle-laboratory Zenobia plots with her son Rafi. They finish the building of the Iron Man.

D 5. On Sinbad's ship - the cargo is revealed as the transformed baboon.

A/D 6. Zenobia and Rafi sail in the bronze boat. The Iron Man kills the Sultan's watchers.
    6A Sultan - Can not do anything about Zenobia   6B attacks of baboon
7. Sinbad arrives off the Island. The journey to Petra.

8. They find the Greek.

D 9. Examination of the baboon and Debate. The only answer is to find and use the powers of The Ultimate Source in Hyperborea - the shrine of the Winter Apollo beyond the North Wind and under the Aurora Borealis.

10. They prepare for the difficult journey north.

A 11. Zenobia follows - anxious to understand more, she goes aboard Sinbad's ship after shrinking herself to a handspan and helped by a sea bird.

A 12. Aboard - Zenobia overhears the Navigation conference and of the two routes through the ice to the Valley of Hyperborea.

A/D 13. She is discovered and nearly killed by the baboon. Her locket containing the means for her re-transformation - a liquid originating from the Ultimate Source - is smashed.

A/D 14. She is examined by the Greek, but manages to escape after he has enlarged a bee with the last of the Source liquid. Zenobia sets the bee to attack the Greek.

A/D 15. Again helped by the sea bird, Zenobia returns to her own vessel. She tells Rafi that they must now be first to the Source so that she may regain her true size and prevent the transformation of the Baboon.

A 16. After the dangers of icebergs, Sinbad arrives in a tundra-like landscape. The main party sets out on foot to traverse the ice and snow.

A/D 17. In the Ice - a giant walrus attacks the camp.

18. They continue and find a frozen mammoth.

19. They reach more temperate country. The Borealis is clear now -

A/D 20. An N man is fighting a giant rhino. Sinbad saves the N man by luring the rhino into a tar pit.

D 21. Through the baboon, they make friends with the N man. He will guide them to the Valley.

22. Zenobia arrives in the Ice Tunnel. They see more creatures frozen into the walls...

23. Sinbad and Company arrive at the Gate to the Valley...

A/D 24. Zenobia approaches the Pyramid. She sets the Iron Man to shift the huge stones to make an entrance. He succeeds, but is smashed to pieces when he slips and brings several blocks down as he falls.

25. Sinbad and Company set out for the distant pyramid.

A 26. Zenobia and Rafi explore the pyramid. They find the Four 'Guardians' and, in the Source, Zenobia recovers her former size.

27. Outside the pyramid, the Greek is alarmed to see the hole. The action of the air on the freezing temperature inside means there's not much time...

A/D 28. They enter. No sign of Zenobia and Rafi, until - without warning - Rafi breaks cover and attacks the baboon. The Baboon kills him. Zenobia - apparently shatterred by the death of her son - appears and is captured without a struggle.

A/D 29. The baboon is transformed into the handsome Prince he was. The Princess embraces him. Zenobia activises the frozen sabre-tooth Tiger.

A/D 30. Sinbad and N man fight the Tiger while the others escape. The N man is killed by the Tiger.

A/D 31. Sinbad at last manages to kill the Tiger.

A 32. Sinbad escapes as the Valley begins to freeze over. The evil Zenobia stays by her dead son. She too begins to turn into a block of ice.

33. By the Valley Gate....Sinbad is reunited with the others. They look back to see the collapse of the pyramid and the end of Hyperborea. It is no more than a legend now - a myth. 'As we will be' concludes the Greek......

1-2 Two pages of Ray's notes based on the early storyline for the project. There are some scenes that don't exist in the final picture but apart from the ending, this simple résumé of the action is as it ended up on the screen. The letters A and D on the left-hand side of the pages indicate whether the scenes would be live-action and/or Dynamation. At the top of the page in Ray's handwriting is 'Funeral Mask of Agamemnon' - presumably this was an idea for an image in the film.

3 A letter dated 9 February 1975 from screenwriter Beverley Cross, the husband of actress Maggie Smith. It is a covering letter that accompanied a revised screenplay, which points out some of the revisions he has made.

4

5

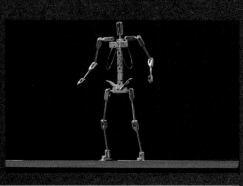

6

7

8

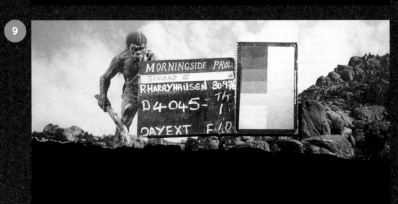

9

10

4 A frame from 35mm test footage showing Ray with the armature for the sabre-toothed tiger and a possible earlier armature, made for *The Golden Voyage of Sinbad*, for an homunculus. By shooting a small amount of footage he would ensure that the armature was going to meet the criteria that he had planned for the full model and that he had a record of the armature.

5 Another frame showing the slate from 35mm footage of the armature for the large baboon that was shot on 14 May 1976, this time specifically for a stills record.

6 The full metal armature for Troglodyte (Trog).

7 Ray animating Trog and the small baboon. The rear-projection image is turned off.

8 A test shot of Trog 'talking' with the small model of the baboon, watched by Pat Wayne, Jane Seymour and others.

9 Another frame from test footage showing the slate dated 30 September 1976. It clearly shows the lower section of the split-screen matted out.

10 Ray animating Trog and the smaller model of the baboon (there were two sizes), with the rear-projection plate turned off and the lower section of the frame matted out. See image 8 for the final combined shot.

1 Photographed in an old aircraft hanger on Malta by gaffer Maurice Gillett, this shows the actors walking over fake rocks in front of a blue screen onto which will be added, by means of a travelling matte, the appropriate background.

2 Also taken in the aircraft hanger, this shows the actors with the blue screen behind for the sequence in front of the huge gates into Hyperborea.

3 Another shot, from a different angle, of the actors on the steps in front of the gates. The gates and scenery that would appear in the gateway were added later by travelling matte.

4 Margaret Whiting and Kurt Christian on part of the deck of the mechanical metal boat. The background, which will again be added in by means of travelling matte, would probably be a miniature set of ice and snow.

5 Ray on the miniature set interior of the pyramid.

6 Another still by Maurice Gillett (as indeed are all the images on these two pages), which shows the crew and actors on the old Malta runway in temperatures that exceeded 100 degrees Fahrenheit. The actors are filming the Walrus sequence (see page 152, image 4) and Ray is sitting on a box by the camera with his back to us.

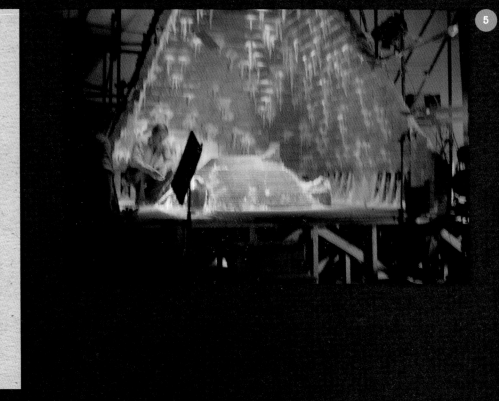

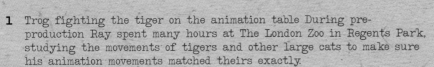

1 Trog fighting the tiger on the animation table During pre-production Ray spent many hours at The London Zoo in Regents Park, studying the movements of tigers and other large cats to make sure his animation movements matched theirs exactly.

2 The armatured giant walrus as he is today. Ray had immense problems animating him as the thick latex covering limited his movements.

3 Four drawings by Ray mounted on cardboard and made before he executed the storyboard for the walrus sequence.

4 The giant walrus as he appears in the film, although this is a test frame. The actors would be choreographed by Ray on the Malta set (see page 151, image 6) and then in the animation studio he would split the screen, just below the walrus' flippers, and animate the walrus model to fit with the choreographed live action.

5 Ray on the ice set built on the Malta runway with a mock-up of the walrus, which gave the actors an idea of what they were fighting.

6 In this shot the models of Trog and the small baboon are climbing the steps up to the gates of Hyperborea. The miniature steps and models are being animated against a blue screen so they can be added to the miniature set of the gates and also the live actors, who had also been shot against a blue screen.

7 The model of Trog reacting to one of the actors on the rear-projection screen. He is standing on the animation table with the lower matte below him.

8 The same pose as in image 7 but from a different angle. The slanted animation table is now clear, as are the fixing screws for Trog under the table.

9 A close-up of the Trog model as he appears in the previous two shots.

Chapter 5

Gods and Titans

Ray is perhaps best known for his classical mythological productions but only two out of the sixteen features he made were truly based on stories from classical Greece. However, in this chapter we cover five projects, three of which were realized (*The 3 Worlds of Gulliver*, *Jason and the Argonauts* and *Clash of the Titans*) and two that were not (*The Satyr* and *Force of the Trojans*). Thoughts of the classical world really began when Ray and his producer, Charles Schneer, were filming *Mysterious Island*. During production they had considered creating a version of the story of Perseus, and at the same time Ray made some notes about a mythological story to which he gave the title *Sinbad in the Age of Muses*. For various reasons they were unable to bring these projects to fruition but Ray was determined that they should make a Greek saga, so he executed some drawings for the story of Jason and his search with the Argonauts for the famed Golden Fleece. His idea of combining Sinbad and Jason in *Sinbad in the Age of Muses* was fortunately dropped in favour of a purer version of the legend.

The Satyr (1940s)

This unrealized project dates from about 1946, after Ray had returned from his post-war travels, which included Mexico. The Yucatán pyramids had impressed him so much that he wrote a rough step outline, which told of an expedition into deep caverns under the pyramids that lead to a legendary underworld where all types of mythological creatures dwell, including a huge Satyr. Unwittingly the expedition members unleash the Satyr into our world. Originating in Greek mythology, satyrs were portrayed as subversive and dangerous, but the Romans made them goat-like from the haunches to the hooves and gave them horns. In the King James Bible they are described as 'hairy ones' and a type of demon or supernatural being. It was a perfect creature for Ray's vivid imagination and it is regretful that the project was never filmed.

1

BLAST HILLSIDE HUGE STONE HEADS ROLL DOWN HILLSIDE

FIGHT WITH MYTHOLOGICAL creature (Griffen)

1 All the sketches on these two pages are dated mid-to-late-1940s. Here the Satyr struggles with a giant snake.

2 This rough sketch depicts the opening of the picture, in which the explorers blast the side of a hill and huge stone Cyclopean heads tumble down the hill.

3 The top sketch shows the Satyr fighting a Griffen; below is a sketch of caves that would lead to – or be part of – the underworld

4 Ray even wanted to get prehistoric creatures into the fray. Here a pterodactyl picks up a human much like a similar creature would in *One Million Years B.C.*

5 Another more detailed sketch of a Griffen, fighting with humans.

6 This very rough sketch depicts what was to have been the first appearance of the Satyr.

The 3 Worlds of Gulliver (1959)

You might wonder why this film has been included in this chapter. In fact Jonathan Swift's satirical story of 1726 fits here rather well as it is all about control of mere mortals. The three worlds that give the film its title are the ordinary world in which we live; the tiny worlds of Lilliput and Blefuscu, in which Gulliver is seen as a god-like figure; and finally the world of Brobdingnag where Gulliver is dwarfed by the inhabitants and seen as a toy, much like the Greek gods played with mortals to amuse themselves. Ray was responsible for the two animation scenes in the film (an inquisitive squirrel and Gulliver's fight with a nasty alligator), a number of complex travelling mattes and the perspective photography that would bring realism to Gulliver's adventures. This is one of Ray's least-known films, possibly because of the small number of animation sequences, but the special effects are a work of genius.

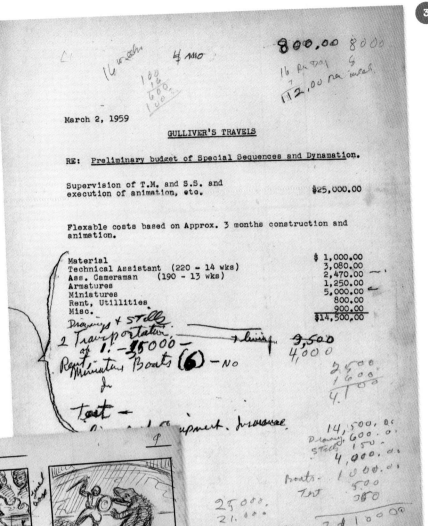

March 2, 1959

GULLIVER'S TRAVELS

RE: Preliminary budget of Special Sequences and Dynamation.

Supervision of T.M. and S.S. and
execution of animation, etc. $25,000.00

Flexable costs based on Approx. 3 months construction and
animation.

Material	$ 1,000.00
Technical Assistant (220 - 14 wks)	3,080.00
Ass. Cameraman (190 - 13 wks)	2,470.00
Armatures	1,250.00
Miniatures	5,000.00
Rent, Utilities	800.00
Misc.	900.00
	$14,500.00

1-2 Two pages of the storyboard for Gulliver's fight with the alligator. They illustrate how Ray planned everything in meticulous detail as most, if not all, of the storyboard is seen in the final film.

3 Ray's preliminary special effects and Dynamation budget dated 2 March 1959. At this stage the budget for optical travelling mattes and animation was $25,000. Ray has handwritten a requirement for six miniature boats, against which either he, or producer Charles Schneer, has later written a definite 'NO'.

4 A comparison sketch showing the relative sizes of characters in the film. There were two sizes for Gulliver, one for a Lilliputian and one for the giant girl Glumdalclitch. This simple sketch helped Ray and the actors to visualize what they would be looking at.

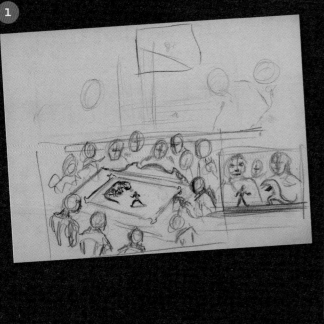

1 Very rough sketches of the fight between Gulliver and the alligator. In the right-hand image the alligator is rearing up and resembles a dinosaur.

2 Ray's first idea was to have Gulliver fight a rat but because Charles Schneer didn't like rats and thought the audience wouldn't either, Ray changed it to an alligator. This is a preliminary sketch for the unleashing of a rat.

3-4 Art Director Gil Parrondo (who appears in the credits as Gil Parrendo), posing on the recce in Spain for two shots that will appear in the final film.

5 Kerwin Mathews, who played Gulliver, alongside Ray, who has a copy of the script in his hand. They are on the S'Agaró beach on the Costa Brava, waiting for the crew to set up the next shot.

6 Ray, who looks very thin after a bad bout of dysentery, talking with Sherry Alberoni (Sherri Alberoni in the credits) and Kerwin Mathews.

7 June Thorburn and Kerwin, standing on the large chess set built in the Studio Verona. This scene would appear in the Brobdingnag section of the film.

8 A wide shot of the chess set taken from the gantry by gaffer Maurice 'Mo' Gillett.

9 Another shot of Kerwin and June taken on the chess set.

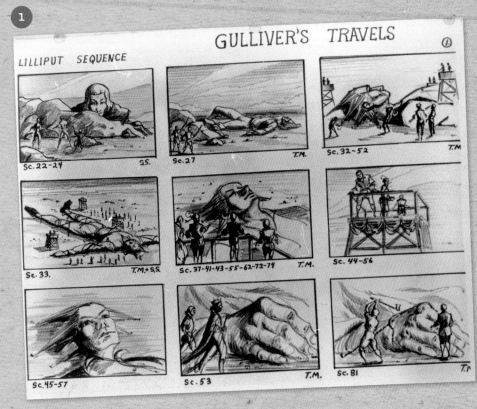

GULLIVER'S TRAVELS

LILLIPUT SEQUENCE

Sc. 22-24   S.S.
Sc. 27   T.M.
Sc. 32-52   T.M.
Sc. 33.   T.M.+S.S.
Sc. 37-41-43-55-62-72-74   T.M.
Sc. 44-56
Sc. 45-57
Sc. 53   T.M.
Sc. 81   T.P.

1 A page of Ray's storyboard for the arrival of Gulliver on Lilliput. He has indicated which shots would be travelling mattes (TM) and which split screen (SS).

2 Kerwin Mathews tied down with miniature ropes and stakes. Either side of him are two miniature platforms, on one of which Ray – who is sitting on the beach on the left – has placed miniature figures.

3 Kerwin spent several hot hours tied to this raised rostrum platform. It was used to track along Gulliver's body for a travelling matte shot.

4 Ray with the 'delightful and extremely talented' June Thorburn, photographed at the Sevilla Studios. Sadly June died in a plane crash in November 1967, just seven years after this picture was taken.

5 The crew setting up a shot for the platform live-action. In the final film these shots would be intercut with the setup in image 2 on page 162.

6 Photographed at the Sevilla Studios, this shows the crew and some actors, including Basil Sydney, filming the scene in which Gulliver kneels in the courtyard of the Emperor's palace.

7 Shot in forced perspective, this picture shows how Gulliver was able to talk with the live actors. The camera is on the left, Kerwin kneels on the right and off down the beach is Lee Patterson and others, standing on the full-size platform. When filmed it would appear as if Kerwin was talking to the other actors even though they were perhaps 30 or 40 yards apart.

Jason and the Argonauts (1963)

A great many people consider this classical Greek adventure a landmark within all the landmarks of Ray's extraordinary career. Although he had to change elements of all his classical films to make them cinematically exciting and avoid problems with the censors, much of the original Jason tale is retained in the film.

It is difficult to believe today that when *Jason* was first released, it was far from successful. This is probably because it was typecast with those poorly made Italian sword and sandal movies, which had begun to fade into obscurity by this time, and to which it is superior in every way. *Jason* is one of Ray's favourite films and he considers it to be his most complete.

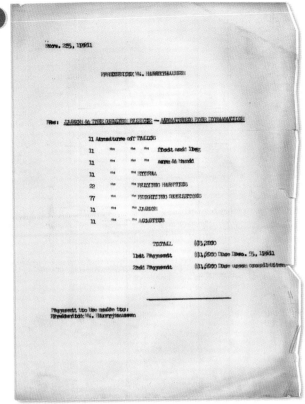

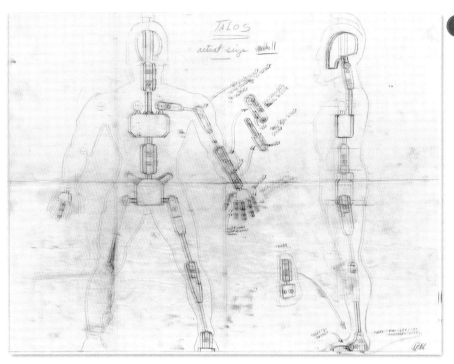

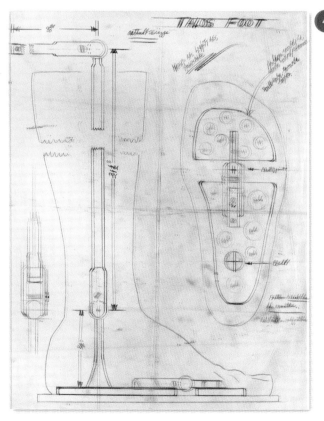

1 Dated 25 November 1961, this is an estimate sent by Fred Harryhausen to his son in England for the construction of the various armatures for *Jason and the Golden Fleece*, which became *Jason and the Argonauts*. Based on Ray's drawings for the armatures the total cost was to be $3,200!

2 The original armature design for Talos that Ray sent to his father so that he could carry out the construction. The design includes detailed instructions.

3 The armature for the foot and heel of Talos, which is 12 inches in length, and the armature for Talos' hand. This was used to reach through the rock arch on the beach and is 10 inches in length. Both artifacts were found in the LA garage.

4 The original armature design for the foot and heel of Talos. Ray has written a note to his father near the top which says 'Keep as light as possible'.

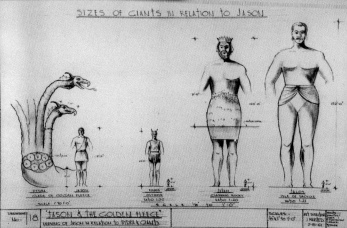

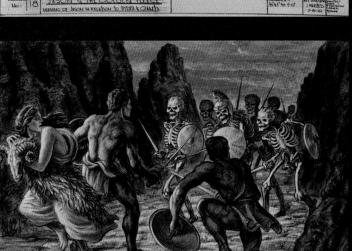

1   A drawing by the art director Jack Maxsted, made to illustrate the cinematic dimensions for Talos, Triton, Hermes and the Hydra in comparison to Jason. All the measurements would have been supplied by Ray, and Jack would have built sets that corresponded with them.

2   Ray's key drawing for The Gateway to the Gods, Mount Olympus. This is an unrealized scene in which Hermes, now fully grown into a god, has flown Jason to Olympus in a fiery chariot.

3   Ray's key drawing for the scene in which Jason faces the seven skeleton warriors. Note that in this drawing the skeletons don't have painted shields.

4   Another unrealized scene. Here Jason and Medea are faced with Cerberus, the two-headed (in mythology it was three) guardian of the underworld. The idea was dropped when Ray had trouble getting the creature to look believable.

5   A hard rubber prototype of Cerberus, which convinced Ray that it wouldn't work.

6   Four pages of the storyboard for Jason's fight with the Hydra and its death. Most of these shots are to be seen in the sequence except for Scene 560, where we see Jason kicking one of the heads.

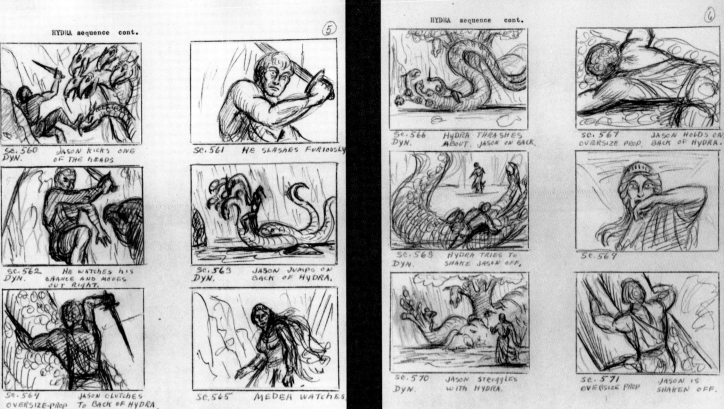

HYDRA sequence cont. ⑤

Sc.560 DYN. JASON KICKS ONE OF THE HEADS

Sc.561 HE SLASHES FURIOUSLY

Sc.562 DYN. HE WATCHES HIS CHANCE AND MOVES OUT RIGHT.

Sc.563 DYN. JASON JUMPS ON BACK OF HYDRA.

Sc.564 OVERSIZE-PROP JASON CLUTCHES TO BACK OF HYDRA.

Sc.565 MEDEA WATCHES

HYDRA sequence cont. ⑥

Sc.566 DYN. HYDRA THRASHES ABOUT. JASON ON BACK.

Sc.567 OVERSIZE PROP. JASON HOLDS ON BACK OF HYDRA.

Sc.568 DYN. HYDRA TRIES TO SHAKE JASON OFF.

Sc.569

Sc.570 DYN. JASON STRUGGLES WITH HYDRA.

Sc.571 OVERSIZE PROP. JASON IS SHAKEN OFF.

HYDRA sequence cont. ⑦

Sc.572 DYN. JASON FALLS TO GROUND.

Sc.573 DYN-TM. HYDRA MOVES CLOSER

Sc.574 DYN. JASON RUNS HIS SWORD INTO HYDRA.

Sc.575 HE MOVES OUT RIGHT OF PICTURE

Sc.576 DYN. HYDRA IN DEATH THROWS.

Sc.577-579-581

HYDRA sequence cont. ⑧

Sc.578 DYN. A BOLT OF LIGHTNING STRIKES THE HYDRA.

Sc.580 DYN. HYDRA IS A MASS OF FLAME.

Sc.582 OVERSIZE PROPS. IN SECONDS THE HYDRA IS REDUCED TO A SKELETON.

Sc.585 JASON FINALLY GETS THE FLEECE

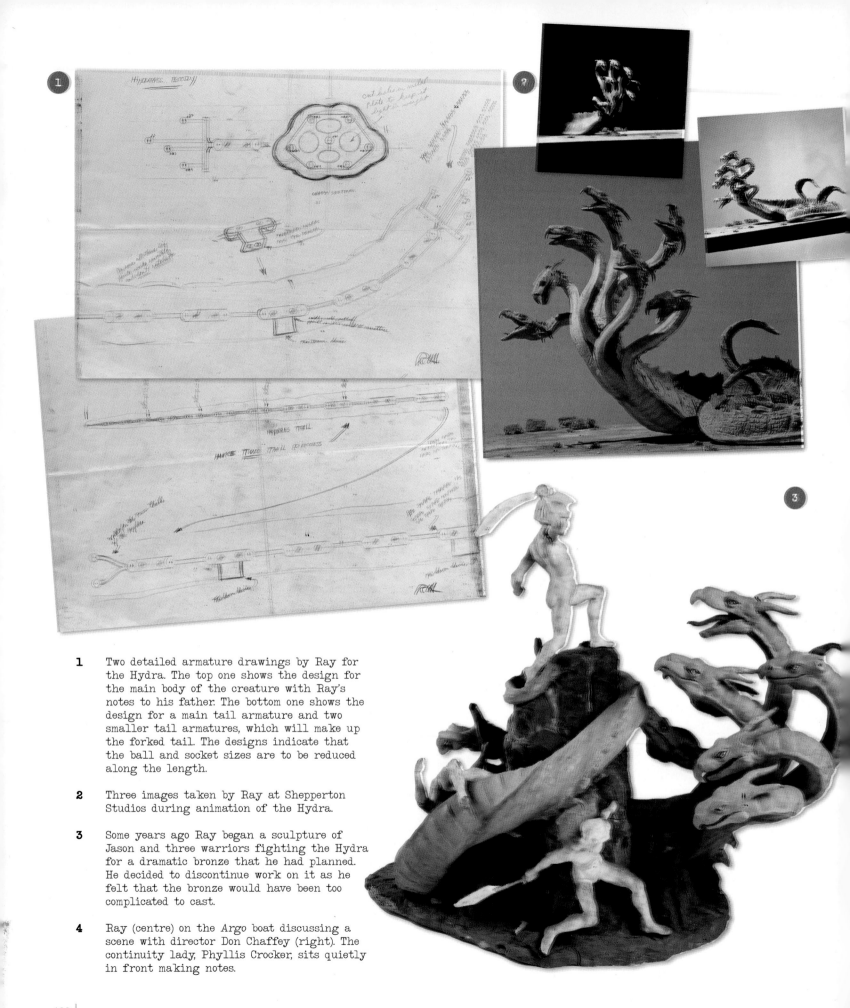

1   Two detailed armature drawings by Ray for
    the Hydra. The top one shows the design for
    the main body of the creature with Ray's
    notes to his father. The bottom one shows the
    design for a main tail armature and two
    smaller tail armatures, which will make up
    the forked tail. The designs indicate that
    the ball and socket sizes are to be reduced
    along the length.

2   Three images taken by Ray at Shepperton
    Studios during animation of the Hydra.

3   Some years ago Ray began a sculpture of
    Jason and three warriors fighting the Hydra
    for a dramatic bronze that he had planned.
    He decided to discontinue work on it as he
    felt that the bronze would have been too
    complicated to cast.

4   Ray (centre) on the *Argo* boat discussing a
    scene with director Don Chaffey (right). The
    continuity lady, Phyllis Crocker, sits quietly
    in front making notes.

5   Ray (centre) with Charles Schneer (right) on board the
    Argo, with two Columbia studio executives.

6   Don Chaffey, leaning against the *Argo*'s side, is talking
    with Todd Armstrong, who has his arms crossed.

7   Fernando Poggi (left), who was uncredited on the film
    and who played Castor and arranged all the incredible
    swordfights, is seen here on the deck of the *Argo* with
    actor Gary Raymond.

8   The crew set up for the live-action photography that will be
    used for the appearance of the skeletons from the ground.

9   Stuntmen rehearse the skeleton fight with Todd Armstrong,
    Andrew Faulds and Fernando Poggi. Each stuntman wore a
    numbered shirt so that when he was animating, Ray could
    see which skeleton was fighting which warrior.

10 Todd Armstrong leaping from a wooden ramp. The action
    takes place at the end of the movie where Todd appears to
    leap over the cliff edge chased by skeletons.

11 Another unfinished (and now brittle) clay sculpture by
    Ray, of Talos kneeling on the bronze plinth. The wooden
    plinth was also made by Ray.

1   On the set for the encounter between Jason and
    Hermes, several of the stuntmen are listening to
    Poggi (in shirt No 2), who would be describing some of
    the swordplay for the skeleton fight sequence.

2   On the miniature set for the Clashing Rocks at
    Shepperton Studios. A technician can be seen top left
    and behind the beautifully made miniature of the
    Argo can just be seen, with his head above water, Bill

Gungeon, the ex-heavyweight boxing champion of Toronto
and former football star, who played the sea god Triton.

3   Stuntmen dressed as Argonauts let down the netting
    over Phineas' temple to enable them to catch the
    Harpies. This sequence was filmed in and around the
    temples at Paestum in Southern Italy.

4   A shot of the men stretching the netting over the
    roof of the temple.

5 Todd Armstrong, Andrew Faulds and Fernando Poggi on the full-size plinth from which the three would fight the skeletons. This shows them fighting blind, or shadow boxing, with the yet to be added skeletons.

6 Stuntman No 4 is pushed by Todd away from the plinth. The action footage with the numbered stuntmen, shot in black and white, was used as a guide by Ray for his animation. For the live-action rear-projection plate, the actors would reshoot the same action as had been choreographed with the stuntmen, this time in colour.

7 Poggi fighting one of the other stuntmen.

8 King Aeetes (Jack Gwillim) holds the helmet containing the Hydra's teeth. He is about to cast them on the ground and evoke the children of the Hydra's teeth: the warrior skeletons.

9 The stuntmen advance on Todd Armstrong, Andrew Faulds and Fernando Poggi.

10 This actually precedes image 9 as it shows the stuntmen standing still, facing the actors just before Jack Gwillim shouts 'Kill Kill Kill them all'.

11 Taken from a different angle this shows the stuntmen charging Jason and his men.

1 One of several recently rediscovered and restored first-generation test images, shot by Ray. The actors on the full-size plinth, obscured here by the miniature one for animation, are slightly soft, due mainly to their movement. In contrast the skeletons are sharp and can now be seen in detail.

2 Another restored test image, which shows in detail the skeletons' shields. It has been suggested that the patterns on these shields reflect Ray's creatures – an octopus, Medusa etc. – but they were based on Greek designs.

3 At first sight this seems like a blurred image of the skeletons, behind which are Jack Gwillim and his soldiers. However, looked at more closely it shows the rear-projection screen and the animation area. The ties for the screen are top left inside the sprocket holes. The table area, on which the model skeletons were animated, is partially visible on the left as it juts out from the main frame of film.

4 A restored test shot of Talos appearing around the side of the cliff and looking down at the terrified Argonauts. Again, this image would have been shot at the time of animation and therefore contains much detail.

5 A final restored test shot of the Harpies trapped inside the temple netting.

6 One of the two Harpy heads thought to have been lost but rediscovered in LA. It isn't in good condition but for the first time, the facial details are revealed.

7 Todd Armstrong in full costume, photographed at the Palentino Studios in Rome. Ray had this taken for reference so that he could make a small model of Todd for the Hydra sequence.

8 Another image, this time of Gary Raymond in costume, that would be used for model construction for the Hydra sequence.

9 Ray sitting with the second unit crew photographing a sequence with Laurence Naismith for the Clashing Rocks sequence. The camera is mounted on a specially rigged platform on the prow of the full-size ship.

10 Ray with director Don Chaffey during location filming in Italy.

Clash of the Titans (1981)

After the success of the Sinbad films and the recognition, by the late 1970s, of *Jason and the Argonauts* as a film classic, Ray and producer Charles Schneer thought it was time to create another Greek adventure. Screenwriter Beverley Cross developed the premise of the story, which incorporated Perseus, a Greek adventurer; a sea monster called the Kraken; the satyr-like Calibos; Pegasus, the winged horse; the Gorgon Medusa; and various other creatures. To find funding Ray made a bronze of Perseus about to behead Medusa and he and Charles hauled this, the screenplay and key drawings around Hollywood. Although Columbia, with whom Ray and Charles had made most of their features, turned the project down as too expensive, MGM accepted and the film was given a $16 million budget, which exceeded the combined budgets of all the pictures Ray had made with Charles.

First Draft Screenplay
December 1977

THE MOON RIDER (working title)

An Original Screenplay
by
BEVERLEY CROSS

The Property of:
ANDOR FILMS LTD.,

2 3 NOV 1977

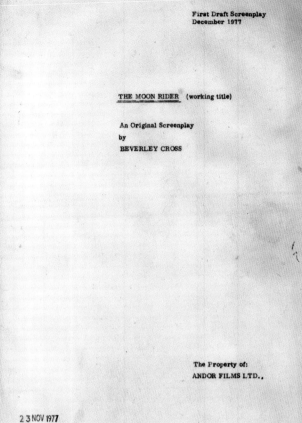

Oct. 2, 1978

Dear Charles:

Enclosed are the "long awaited" drawings. They include the SCORPION SEQUENCE and the FLOOD SEQUENCE. I have copies for my script and enclose the originals for the copying and inclusion in the necessary other scripts.

The miniature sets for the FLOOD SEQUENCE will have to be about 4 feet high because of the water problem. They will have to be built to collapse on cue. A substantial dump tank or tanks will be required. All miniatures can be shot outside of the large tank in Malta with the exception of Sc. 29 and 30.   For these two shots the same miniature background could be used although additions would have to be made for Sc. 30.   Use of "cut outs" could be used in far background.   Some kind of fog machine will be necessary on all models to help give a sense of distance and perspective. Needless to say a second camera would perhaps pick up necessary close ups at the same time.

The TM situation is rather grim, costwise.   I received a phone call last Friday from MPI and will forward their letter when I receive it.   To save time I'll mail the drawings today.   Costs are as follows.

  $1,600 per shot
     250 for auxillary and surround matts, when needed.
     250 for double TM

     1/3 payment down in advance

     10 to 15 day delivery depending on complications of shots.   Would help to deliver several shots at once.

I talked to Lynn Dunn of FILM EFFECTS on the phone and his figures are about the same in the long run.

     Average length of shot 20 - 25 feet.
     About $1,500 per shot
     $10 per foot additional.
     Auxillary mattes or double TM additional.

     Could go up to $2,000 per shot depending on complications.

It would appear all companies here are about the same, cost wise.   Howard Anderson would perhaps be a little less expensive.   When the time comes groups of shots of 10 - 15 could be distributed to different companies including the one British company you mentioned.   Anyway the above will give you an idea of what to budget for if the elements are put together in Hollywood.

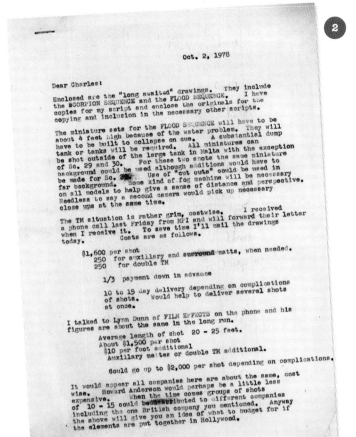

THE KRAKAN

1   The front page of a recently found early screenplay for *Clash of the Titans*, dated 23 November 1977. It was then called *The Moon Rider*, a title Ray had not recalled when we wrote our 2003 book *An Animated Life*.

2   The first page of a memo from Ray to Charles, dated 2 October 1978. It details problems with various sequences and travelling mattes. The quotes from various effects companies were high, and in the end another optical technician, Frank Van der Veer, worked on the travelling mattes.

3   One of the earliest sketches of Medusa, probably executed in 1977/8. At this stage Ray was trying to decide whether to show her breasts or depict her with a see-through bra, or as he calls it, a 'boob tube'. At the time Ray didn't want to get an X-rating.

4   A comparison drawing for the Kraken, the Titan of the title. Ray's estimation of how high it would appear on the screen is on the left-hand side and reads '40 feet'.

1 An estimate from Colin Arthur, dated 18 October 1978, for special makeup and large live-action models of certain items in the screenplay. He mentions a giant hand from which Perseus steps, which at some point must have been in a version of the script. Colin did go on to work on the picture and supplied the special makeup for Neil McCarthy as the live-action Calibos and the underwater version of the Kraken, which he built in the front room of his house.

2 A costing from Colin for the production wigs.

3 Ray's drawing for the giant vulture in which he also places Andromeda to show the relative size.

4 Two head drawings of Medusa and two drawings of the blind Stygian witches.

5 The key drawing for the Kraken.

6 Although badly damaged this is Ray's original armature drawing for Dioskilos, the two-headed guardian. The joint for the two ball and socket armatures needed for the creature's heads is sketched just above where it will be located.

7 The original armature drawing for Pegasus, complete with Ray's instructions.

8 Another original armature drawing, this time for Calibos. Up until 1964 Ray's father made all his armatures and as the two had such a close understanding, it wasn't necessary to make so many notes. After that time Ray employed various companies to make the armatures, so he needed to make sure that everything was as he wanted.

9 An unfinished clay maquette by Ray that was to have been for a bronze of Calibos.

10 Another unfinished clay maquette, this time depicting the Stygian witches reaching up to Perseus, who holds their eye. This would have been the first stage only of construction as Perseus and the witches have no features.

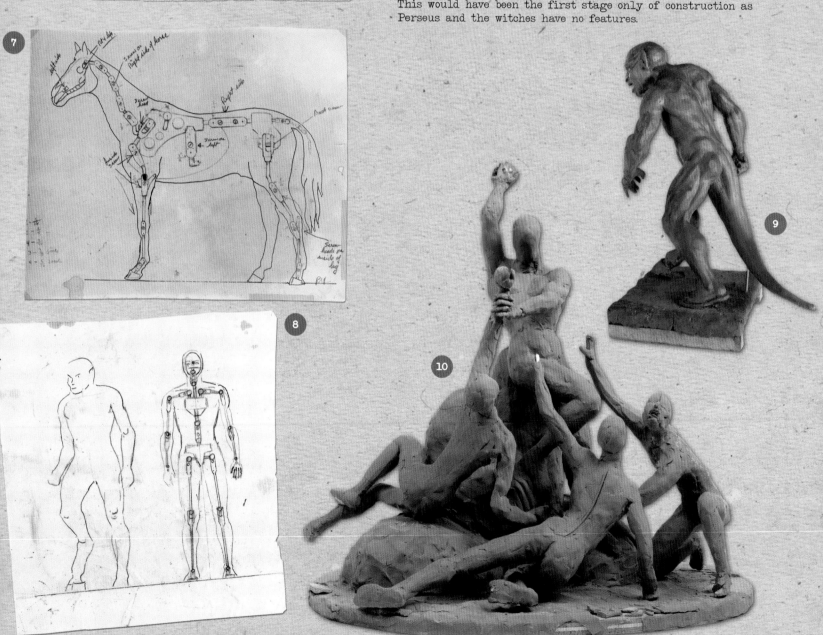

1 Five pages of the storyboard for the capture of
   Pegasus. They depict various scenes, all of which are
   featured in the final cut, as well as Ray's scene
   descriptions and notes. Ray typed all his notes
   on his own portable typewriter, which is now in
   the collection of the Ray and Diana Harryhausen
   Foundation.

2 Page 48 from the screenplay, which relates the
   appearance of Pegasus in the Wells of the Moon.

GOZO - MALTA   Procession Sc 602 part

procession Sc 602 part

Procession Sc 602 part 630

617 625   PART- 629

procession Sc 602 part.

reverses Procession Sc 602 part

L S reverses 603 part, 612

L S reverses 603p 612

POSSIBLE 619 PLATE

MALTA - NR. STUDIO   SC 600, 594, 111

3 Two sets of location recce photographs taken at Gozo on Malta, on which Ray has sketched ideas for the Kraken sequence and the rescue of Andromeda by Perseus and Pegasus. Other locations were in Italy and Spain.

4 One of a set of beautiful renditions by R.L. Allen for a comic book based on the film, this one showing the encounter between Perseus and Dioskilos.

1 The small studio where Ray worked whilst making *Clash of the Titans* at Pinewood Studios in Buckinghamshire, England. Ray's Jaguar car is standing outside. When we visited Pinewood in the 1990s we made a detour to look at this area and it was still being used for special effects.

2 A full clay rendition of Medusa, photographed in Ray's London study.

3 Pegasus, Calibos and one of the skeletons patiently wait in Ray's Pinewood studio area.

4 An early plaster head of Medusa, which was rejected by Ray as the snakes were too small. He always wanted to use red eyes but rather disappointingly couldn't find any red doll's eyes, so in the end he used blue. It could be said perhaps that after Aphrodite turned her into a Gorgon the eyes became the last vestige of her lost beauty?

5 The armatured model of Medusa that was used in the film, also waiting to be animated. Here we can see the blue eyes.

6 A close-up of the large model of Calibos.

7 Dioskilos, a model of Perseus, one of the two models of Pegasus and one of the giant scorpions. Ray took these pictures during animation to record in detail what they looked like when constructed.

8 The Kraken turned to stone. These two models were used to show the Kraken crumbling into the sea after Perseus holds up the head of Medusa.

9 Ray ensuring an animation shot is exactly how he wanted it. On this production Ray was assisted by two excellent animators – Jim Danforth and Steve Archer. Because of various earlier problems with film stock, Ray had to concede that he needed help to complete the production on time. As these were his creations he had to make sure that Jim and Steve were following his vision when it came to animation.

10 Animator Steve Archer working on the Kraken sequence.

11 The Kraken lusting over Andromeda. It was never quite clear how he was to have disentangled her from her chains.

12 This is a test for stills of the exact same scene as shown in image 11 and shows the matted-out area where the rocks would be. Ray is holding the piece of paper.

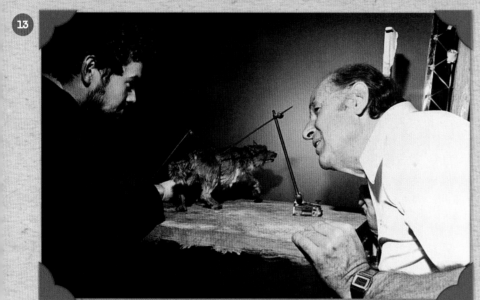

1 Animator and friend Jim Danforth during the animation of the taming of Pegasus by Perseus. This was shot against a blue screen and the models were held in place by a rod, covered in a V of blue-screen material, which can just be made out below the models.

2 Ray and an assistant working with the very large torso and head of the Kraken, possibly for the appearance of the Titan from the sea.

3 The large model of Calibos waiting to be placed on the animation table for the scorpion scenes in which he is 'killed'. On the rear-projection screen is a frame of the live-action footage.

4 A member of the crew working in part of the chaotic animation area, where we can see Ray's wooden-framed rear-projection screens.

5 Another shot of the large Kraken model, about to be photographed as it emerges from the sea.

6 Perseus struggles to remain on Pegasus' back as the creature bucks in its struggle not to be tamed. The models can be seen against the blue screen onto which will be optically added real clouds and sky.

7 Taken by Ray this is a rare photograph of Laurence Olivier as Zeus during the live-action photography at Pinewood Studios. Olivier sits in his throne in the background with the camera behind him. Charles Schneer is looking directly at the camera.

8 Ray looking through the viewfinder on his Mitchell camera.

9 Neil McCarthy as the live-action Calibos, being made up by Colin Arthur and Basil Newall. Basil was chief makeup artist on the film whilst Colin was head of SFX makeup.

10 The beautiful model of Dioskilos on the animation table.

11 The large upper torso of the Kraken. This together with 2 and 5 are probably images of the high-speed photography that would show the creature rising out of the sea.

12 A beautiful, recently discovered shot of Ray posing for the camera during animation. He is leaning on one of his rear projectors, possibly the oldest, dating from the 1920s.

13 On the left is Steve Archer discussing a pose with Ray. On the animation table can be seen Dioskilos and two surface gauges, which were used to help the animator to work out how far to move the model.

14 Another recently discovered shot of Ray, in the animation studio during the animation for the Kraken rising out of the sea. The camera and tripod can be seen clearly, as can the rear-projection screen.

Force of the Trojans (1980-81)

Clash of the Titans proved to be a worldwide success, so Ray, producer Charles Schneer and screenwriter Beverley Cross searched for another classic legend and found it in the journey of Aeneas from Troy to found Rome. Along the way he would encounter various characters and creatures, amongst which were the fatal flight of Icarus, a colony of Cyclops, Furies, jackal men, the Sphinx of Phryria, the evil goddess Hecate, and Scylla and Charybdis (a mutation of octopus, triton and sea serpent). MGM, who had commissioned *Clash of the Titans*, agreed to finance the development of the screenplay, a recce for locations and preparations for the Dynamation sequences.

In the event the production languished, perhaps because this type of picture, with its clean-cut hero, heroine, evil and benign gods, and fantastic creatures, had succumbed to the dark comic book style of the anti-hero. All that remains of the project is an excellent screenplay by Beverley, Ray's rough sketches and his clay figure of the Sphinx.

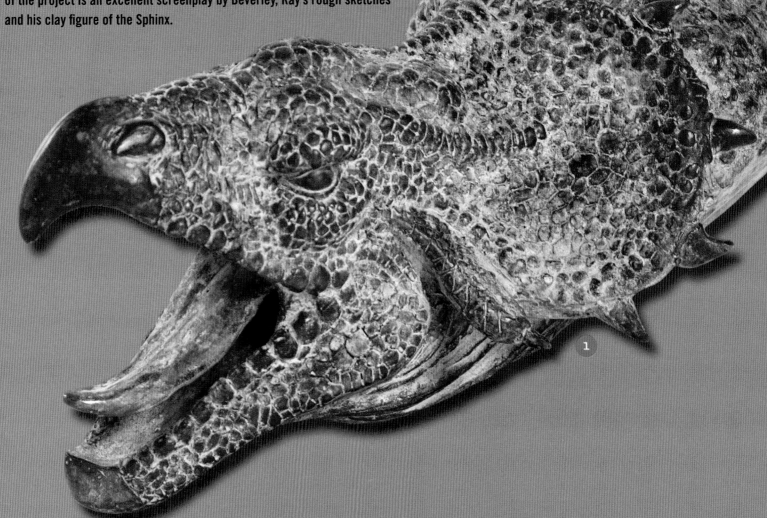

1 The head of Ray's bronze of Scylla, a creature that would have been featured in *Force of the Trojans*.

2 Ray, Charles and Beverley visited a number of locations during the recce for *Force of the Trojans*. Here is Ray on the left in Giza, Egypt, in front of (left to right) the pyramids of Menkaure, Cheops or Khufu and Chephren or Khafre, all of which would have featured in the storyline for the film.

3 Another possible location, this time across the Nile from Luxor at the Ramesseum. This shows the colossal statue of the pharaoh Ramesses, which collapsed millennia ago and on which the poet Shelley based his sonnet 'Ozymandias'. As Ray has taken this image he is not to be seen but Beverley Cross, the screenwriter, is on the right of the picture below the collapsed statue.

4 A wonderful set of sketches by Ray, which we found in an old sketch book, of various ideas for the Cyclopses that would have hopefully featured in the film.

5 A sketch for the first appearance of a Cyclops. He sports a beard and fang-like teeth. Unlike the Cyclops in *The 7th Voyage of Sinbad*, he does not have cloven hooves.

6 Another page of sketches and doodles, this time showing Sirens, which Ray portrayed as mermaid-like creatures.

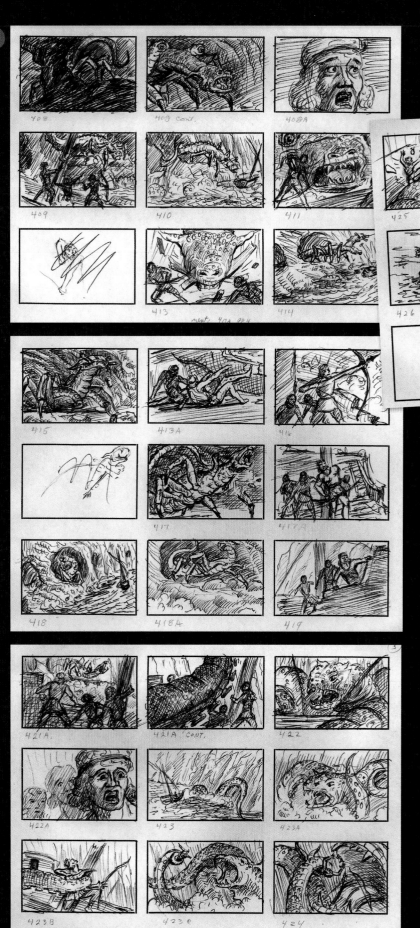

1 Four pages of a rough storyboard for the
   Scylla and Charybdis sequence in the
   screenplay. In the story Aeneas' ship is
   attacked first by Charybdis, which emerges
   from a cave and then by the tentacled
   Scylla, which pulls the ship and occupants
   under, much like the octopus did in *It
   Came From Beneath the Sea*. However, if this
   sequence had been filmed it would have
   been much superior to that of the earlier
   movie.

2 Another sketch (there were never any key
   drawings made for the project), this time
   showing the Sphinx attacking Aeneas and
   his companions. It is possible that this
   creature might have rivalled even Medusa
   as one of Ray's most hideous creations.

3 Ray's clay model of the Sphinx as it would
   have appeared in the film. This was sadly
   never made into a metal and latex model.

Acknowledgements

As always, we are indebted to many people and organizations for their cooperation and generosity in allowing us to use images and helping with the compilation of this volume.

Colin Arthur

The British Academy of Film and Television Arts (BAFTA)

The British Film Institute (BFI)

Canal + UK Ltd

Mark Caballero

Randy Cook – a million thanks to Randy for all his advice and support during the years that we have been friends.

Matilda Cook

Grover Crisp

Jim Danforth

Alan Friswell

Maurice Gillett and his family

Terry Gilliam

Hammer Films

Vanessa Harryhausen

Peter Jackson

Andy Johnson – one of the three photographers who worked on this book and who has become a dear friend.

Wayne Kirk

John Landis – who has been a good friend to Ray and is always so willing to help in any way he can.

The London Film Museum – all the staff and technicians especially Jonathan Sands, Leslie Hardcastle, Lucy and Linda Ayton and Steve Perdue.

James Mansfield

Mark Mawston

Karl Meyer – Gentle Giant Studios

Tim Nicholson – for his long-suffering ability to listen about everything Harryhausen and who has read the text for this and the previous four books.

Sony Pictures

Jeff Taylor

John Ulakovic

Seamus Walsh

Warner Bros

David Whistance

And especially The Ray and Diana Harryhausen Foundation, Bobby Birchall, the designer of this book, and Stuart Cooper, the patient editor.

1   Ray receives recognition from friends and filmmakers at his 90th birthday event held at BFI Southbank in London on Saturday 26 June 2010. This event was sponsored by BAFTA and the BFI and was a total surprise to Ray as he thought it was to be a straightforward on-stage talk. Left to right: John Landis (the master of ceremonies), Dennis Muren, Ken Ralston, Peter Jackson, Ray, Rick Baker, Randy Cook and Phil Tippett. All children of the Hydra's teeth.

2   Everyone on stage at the end of the tributes. Left to right: John Landis, David Sproxton, Mark Caballero, Seamus Walsh (behind Mark), Rick Baker, Ken Ralston, Peter Lord, Dennis Muren, Phil Tippett, Tony Dalton, Peter Jackson, John Cairney, Randy Cook, Gary Raymond (behind Randy), Jim Aupperle, Dr Rolf Giesen, Chris Endicott (behind Rolf), Vanessa Harryhausen, Caroline Munro and Nick Park. Ray is centre stage clutching his precious BAFTA award and Colin Arthur kneels next to him.

3   Ray in his study in April 2011. He sits behind the desk at which he created many imaginary sequences and creatures. In front of him is a reproduction armature of Mighty Joe Young, the styracosaurus from *The Valley of Gwangi* and Uguchio, Ray's name for the *Jason and the Argonauts* skeleton that he keeps in his study.

4   The hands that produced so much. In this and the previous picture it can be seen just how large those hands and fingers are.

Index

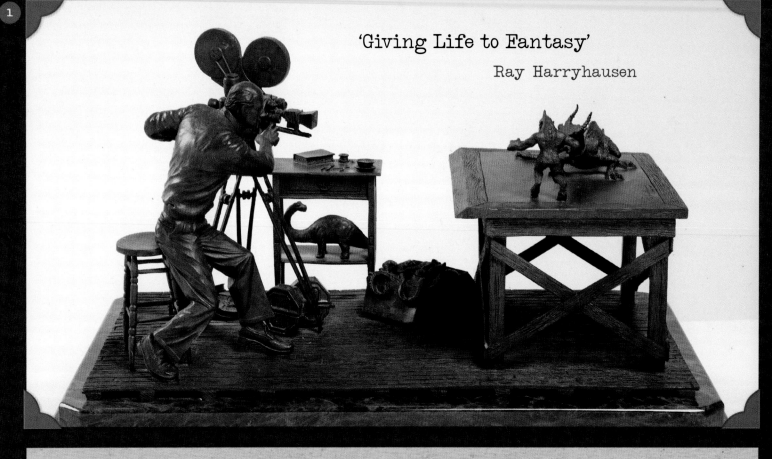

'Giving Life to Fantasy'

Ray Harryhausen

First published in Great Britain 2011
by Aurum Press Ltd
7 Greenland Street
London NW1 0ND
www.aurumpress.co.uk

ISBN 978 1 84513 557 7

Commissioning Editor: Stuart Cooper
Designer: Bobby Birchall, Bobby&Co
Photography: Andy Johnson, Wayne Kirk, Mark Mawston

Printed in Singapore.

Title page photographs
Page 1: Detail from the 'Giving Life to Fantasy' bronze
(shown in full above), designed and executed by Ray
Harryhausen and completed by John Ulakovic.
Page 2: Various items on Ray's desk including the
typewriter on which he typed all of the storyboard notes,
part of the archelon storyboard from *One Million Years B.C.*
and several armatures.
Page 3: One of the three golden masks seen in *The Golden
Voyage of Sinbad*.